THE WASTED HALF

THE WASTED HALF

HOW TO MAXIMIZE YOUR ADVERTISING DOLLAR

John F. Davis

Writer's Showcase

San Jose New York Lincoln Shanghai

The Wasted Half
How To Maximize Your Advertising Dollar

Writer's Showcase
an imprint of iUniverse.com, Inc.

For information address:
iUniverse.com, Inc.
5220 S 16th, Ste. 200
Lincoln, NE 68512
www.iuniverse.com

ISBN: 0-595-18317-4

Printed in the United States of America

"I know half the money I spend on advertising is wasted; I just don't know which half!"

—Joseph Wannamaker

That quote has been attributed to several sources, most often Joseph Wannamaker, whose Philadelphia department store started so many advertising trends. Regardless of whether he or some other advertising professional actually said it, its universality within the industry gives it a veracity that attribution, no matter how distinguished, never could.

This book is about "which half." Advertising agency presidents are probably going to hate it. Creative directors, too. Many marketing vice presidents will fear it. And all for the same reason:

It's the truth.

If you're the CEO of a company that spends a lot of money on advertising, get ready to cut your annual budget. You may even get rid of your advertising agency, or at least replace it. You'll probably improve morale within your company and still get better results. Small advertisers will also find ways to save. And readers who aren't really involved in the business will still find insights into America's most fascinating business.

Advertisers spend $100 billion every year to influence what we buy and how we think. $100 billion! That's big bucks. Even if Joseph Wannamaker is right and half is wasted, $50 billion is nothing to be sneezed at. Remember when candidate George W. Bush shocked the political world by raising $30 million? Chicken feed.

Imagine what could happen to America's economy if that $100 billion were cut in half and the wasted half invested in research and development, used to raise staff salaries and returned to investors. It can be done.

I

There's More To Be Learned
From Advertising's Past Than Its Present.

Advertising, for better or worse, has always been with us. It wasn't until the advent of the printing press, however, that it began to grow into what we know today. The first newspapers ran advertising, usually a page filled with ads and notices one column wide and an inch or two deep. Then advertisers began to notice that their messages were lost among the clutter on the page. Thus began the quest of modern advertising: to deliver the strongest message while avoiding clutter. At first this seemed a simple problem to solve, enlarge the ad, add an illustration and make the type bigger. But, of course, everyone started doing the same thing and the end result was simply larger and livelier clutter.

Enter the advertising agent. I've always have an image of these guys as vigorous entrepreneurs, dressed in striped vests and two-tone shoes and gifted with a persuasive manner and, perhaps, even a little talent. They sold advertising space for publications and lived off a 15 percent commission. In exchange, they worked mightily to produce advertising that stood out from the clutter and delivered their client's message as effectively as possible. Sounds easy, but this was, in fact, a very difficult task. It was a rare individual who could write a terse, yet persuasive headline, render an effective illustration, write text that would assure the reader's continued interest and lay it all out in a manner that was attractive to the eye. As a result, the agent began to turn to other resources, such as the copywriter and the illustrator.

At the same time, clients began to raise questions about which publication would be most effective for their particular products and services. The agents began to see large, and sometimes surprising, responses to the same ad when placed in different publications. Thus arose the media planner and buyer, advertising's first step away from it's flamboyant, gut-feel past into what came to be a more "scientific" approach. With the advent of radio and, later, television, the two most predominant demands of advertising became even stronger:

- Make my message stand out from the clutter.
- Place my message where it is most likely to reach my potential customer.

Much of today's advertising is still floundering around, trying to solve these same basic problems, while valuable lessons go unlearned and opportunities untried.

What was missing in these early days, and still too often is missing, was an overriding concern with what the message conveyed. Advertisers then, as they often still do, assume that an eager audience is out there, trembling with anxiety in anticipation of receiving whatever message they might impart. The fact that it still happens today is apparent in much of the advertising for computers and other "high-tech" products; the advertiser seems fully confident that the consumer not only wants but is crying out for his product, while the consumer he is trying to reach hasn't the faintest idea of what the product is or does and is, for the most part, perfectly satisfied with the way he is currently operating. The high-tech advertiser, usually someone with an inventive mind and an engineering degree but absolutely no grasp of popular culture, goes through a series of advertising agencies, whose own priorities, we will later learn, are far different, all with little or no success. All of this because no one asked a simple question: what message will motivate someone to buy this gadget?

But we are ahead of ourselves.

II

The Fathers of Modern Advertising

Albert Lasker is generally known as the father of modern advertising, mostly because he insisted that advertising copy should sell as well as inform. Doesn't seem like much of a breakthrough now, but at the time he made quite an impression.

Lasker was born in Germany but came to America as an infant. Many immigrants of the time took a look at New York with its teeming hordes of new arrivals and decided to stay on the boat and check out some other ports farther down the coast. The Laskers stayed on until Galveston, Texas, where Albert grew up and graduated high school. In 1898, he came to work in Chicago for Lord and Thomas, an advertising agency that looms large in our story. Seven years later, he became head copywriter. In another seven, he was sole owner of the agency, which, under his leadership became the largest in the world. He introduced the public to such wonders as Kotex and Kleenex and is credited with a campaign for Lucky Strike cigarettes that made it sociably acceptable for women to smoke. He introduced such, at the time, revolutionary ideas as slogans, celebrity endorsements and reliance on images as well as words.

However, his most important contribution to advertising may have been simply hiring one of the best writers to ever find his way into the business, Claude C. Hopkins.

The Birth of "Scientific Advertising"

Hopkins used advertising in an entirely different manner, and his inventiveness changed the way advertising has been done ever since. His methodology is contained in a small volume entitled *Scientific Advertising*. In those days, science was prescribed as the cure for all of the world's ills and Hopkins saw advertising's woes as subject to the same tonic. The book is so small and so readable that I recommend anyone with a real interest in the subject read it. Yes, much of what it says is outdated; but the basic underlying principles are still powerful and still deserve attention from anyone interested in effective advertising.

When I first started in advertising, I was introduced to a standard technique for starting or reviving a consumer product: run an ad with a coupon in a newspaper or magazine and follow it with an ad to the trade informing them of the consumer ad and urging them to stock up on the product in anticipation of wildly increased sales. It was a proven technique that everyone used. Claude Hopkins invented it.

He invented sampling, giving away samples of the product to the potential customer. He invented promotions, once having the "World's Largest Cake" baked and displayed to promote a lard substitute.

But his greatest contributions were to:

(1) Popularize the idea of using common language and specific benefits in advertising and

(2) Focus ads on unique properties of the product.

When Hopkins first came along at the turn of the century (he was born only two years after the end of the Civil War), advertisers competed for the most florid descriptions of their products. "The world's finest" and "no other compares" were among the most common. Hopkins thought ordinary people would be suspicious of such language. Instead he used language that bordered on slang, with fragmented sentences and a style that, he said, met the approval of the consumer if not the literary critic.

Finding a unique benefit in a product was equally revolutionary. Hopkins described most ads as communicating no more than "buy my product rather than my competitors." He proposed to give the consumer a specific and believable reason to buy.

Sometimes, the reasons made perfect sense, such as the campaign for Schlitz Beer that emphasized the cleanliness of their brewing process. Others, such as that for Puffed Rice and Puffed Wheat, had an appeal that today seems more elusive: "Food Shot From Guns!"

Like Lasker, Hopkins insisted that advertising should sell, rather than merely inform, and he urged his clients to think of each ad just he would a salesman; if he fails to produce, fire him and put another in his place.

What's more, he declared, "real salesmanship has no regard for price." Typically, he proved his statement by going out and selling a common household product with no discernible advantages, shortening, at a high price. Want to know how? Read Chapter Six of *My Life in Advertising*. I'm not being coy here, I really want you to read it; it well may give you some exciting ideas of your own about whatever product or service you sell.

A word of warning: do not swallow Claude Hopkins' theories whole. He came along before radio, much less television, and at a time when far fewer Americans were as literate and sophisticated as they are today. Still, his contribution was enormous. He invented couponing and sampling, product testing and no-nonsense copy. He took the writer out of the office and into the manufacturing plants and stores. He took small, unknown products and turned them into category leaders.

Hopkins "scientific" approach also gave birth to a powerful new discipline in advertising, Consumer Research. Public opinion polling was already a growing endeavor and making a huge impact on politics. Later, companies like Gallup and Robinson applied some of the same techniques to advertising, trying to determine the effectiveness of an advertising message by asking the consumer what he or she thought. It sounds good. In fact, it makes perfect sense. The problem with it, in all its many forms, is and has been the assumption that the consumer is going to tell you the truth. A recent survey revealed that the average American lies, on average, seven times a day. What makes us think they don't lie to us?

To illustrate this problem, take the experience of Shell Oil Company in the early 1970's. Shell, like many gasoline retailers, was offering premiums to its customers. If you filled your tank with Shell Gasoline, you could buy a glass or some other premium at very little cost. A vast array of potential premiums was tested by Shell and its advertising agency, Ogilvy and Mather. One of the most popular was a series of children's books. They asked customers if they would like to have these books to enhance their children's education and the customers said yes.

Of course they said yes! What kind of moron is going to look at another person and say , no, I don't give a damn about my kids, I want a glass with my favorite NFL team's emblem on it?

Shell went ahead with the children's books and it was a bomb. This is not to say all consumer research is so poorly conceived. Far from it. But too much reliance on it has proved disastrous more than once.

The successes of consumer research for many products, plus an understandable desire from manufacturers and service providers for something more than a hunch as to whether or not an ad would work, led to a boom in research techniques and options. Research companies sprang up in all the large markets. Then advertising agencies hired their own research people who could both understand and speak the new language of these social scientists and statisticians.

III

A Trio Of Giants

From the emphasis on research arose one of the crankiest, smartest, most opinionated, and likable personalities in the history of the business: an extraordinary British self-promoter named David Ogilvy. Ogilvy, who often admitted owing much of his success in advertising to Hopkins, had trained as a chef in Paris before coming to America to work with the Gallup organization in public opinion research; just one of many head-turning job changes in his life. He was also later identified as an agent of the British Secret Service working within the United States to influence the government and, presumably, the people in favor of entering the war against Nazi Germany. After the war, David started his own agency despite having no clients and no real experience in the business. Where did his start-up cash come from? My guess is from a grateful British nation, but then, who knows?

While his knowledge of how to execute an advertisement may have been lacking, his understanding of how the American public responded to media was not. In addition, David Ogilvy was a true advertising genius.

Most of his work for Gallup was in testing audience reaction to Hollywood films. He felt the same formulas could work for advertised products. Other than that, Ogilvy claimed to have learned the following during those years:

"George Gallup taught me three things of consummate value. One, grant graciously what you dare not refuse. Two, when you don't know the answer, confuse the issue. Three, when you foul the air in somebody else's bathroom, burn a match and the smell will vanish."

The enemy of originality

At the same time that Ogilvy was getting his new agency, Ogilvy and Mather, underway, a new star was rising in the ranks of the Ted Bates Agency, a bright and energetic copywriter named Rosser Reeves. As much as Reeves adored beauty and poetry in art and literature, he despised it in advertising. His no-nonsense approach to the business, in many ways derivative of Hopkins, proved not only effective but extremely appealing to the hard-headed American businessman of the time. Reeves' approach made sense. There was no silly talk about beautiful illustrations and artful copy, just a sensible, down-to-earth approach that any engineer, CPA or business school graduate could get his or her head around. Originality, he declared, is the most dangerous word in advertising. He warned against the egos of copywriters which caused them to value the creativity of the ad over the selling message of the product.

Reeves went on to establish what he called the "Copy Laboratory" at Ted Bates, a place where writers could test the efficacy of their messages. Obviously, he was a great believer in consumer research and insisted that every advertisement be tested. Through his dedication to research he developed one of the most powerful and lasting theories in advertising, the need for the Unique Selling Proposition, or USP. He identified three parts to the use of the USP in advertising.

Every ad must make a single, powerful proposition to the consumer that tells him or her that if you buy this product you will get this specific benefit.

This proposition must be one that the competition either cannot, or does not, offer. It has to be either a unique property of the brand or a claim of effectiveness that no competitor can make.

The USP must be so powerful and appealing that potential consumers feel compelled to try the product or service.

While some of this may seem like so much nonsense in today's world of communication, it led to one very important statement by Reeves in his 1961 book, *Reality In Advertising*. Reeves wrote:

"The consumer tends to remember just one thing from an advertisement—one strong claim or one strong concept."

In this, he departs from Hopkins, who would begin with a unique property but would never limit his copy to it. Believing that once you had the reader's attention, you should deluge him or her with every selling message you could, Hopkins filled the ad with copy. Not Reeves. He delivered the message quickly and powerfully, then stopped.

Importantly, Reeves also said the USP must be a message the consumer takes from the ad, rather than one the copywriter puts into the ad. It worked well for Ted Bates clients that included Wonder Bread (builds strong bodies eight ways), M&M Candies (melt in your mouth, not in your hand), Certs Breath Mints (with a magic drop of Retsyn), and Colgate Toothpaste (cleans your breath as it cleans your teeth).

A candid admission: I took only one advertising course in college and I made a D in it. Usually when I did badly, I retook the course to erase the old grade, but this course was too dreadful to consider taking a second time. It was a basic course in Rosser Reeves' brand of advertising. First you gave your USP (it makes you smell better) and then you prove it with a "reason why" (it contains chlorophyll). What a dull and tedious way to communicate with others. What a degrading way to earn a living. At least, that's how I thought as a college student in the Sixties.

One can immediately see the appeal of such an approach to the practical businessman, however. Not so apparent is its greatest flaw: while Rosser Reeves, to great effect, promoted Fleissman's as "the corn oil margarine," he could do nothing to prevent other manufacturers from turning out their own margarine made from the same stuff and, perhaps, pricing it more attractively. By the time *Reality In Advertising* hit the bookshelves, advertisers were becoming aware of another problem that competed with the old bugaboos of clutter and the difficulty in crafting an effective message: parity products. In short, many if not most of the products on America's shelves were no better or worse— and rarely any different in anything but packaging—from the one on the next shelf. However, our ever-resourceful advertising agent did not let this slow him down.

The USP gave birth to the "pre-emptive claim." This meant boasting about an ingredient that all of your competitors put in their products but, as of yet, had failed to mention. Shell, for example, boasted that their gasoline contained TCP, a chemical agent they pictured in ads dripping from a teaspoon. This small amount of TCP in a gas tank, they asserted, stopped engine knock, hesitation and run-on. In fact it was either the same, or very similar to lead additives used by every oil company. But it, like other pre-emptive claims, was very successful, resulting in an explosion of advertising boasting of magical and secret ingredients that often left the average consumer, if there is such a person, wary and dubious. TCP, my own uncle told me, really stood for Texas Cow Pee.

There wasn't anything really new about the pre-emptive claim. Hopkins had used it to sell shortening back at the turn of the century. But it became the popular method of advertising as we moved into the 1950's, and it was often combined with another technique that tried America's patience with advertising, the "mnemonic device."

Conceived as an aid to memory, the mnemonic device was relatively harmless when it came in the form of a cartoon character such as Tony the Tiger and the Jolly Green Giant, both created along with many others by the Leo Burnett Agency in Chicago. But when it produced white knights galloping down neighborhood streets and tiny men in rowboats adrift in your toilet, it began to make even the most intelligent and resourceful advertising practitioners appear to be morons.

Of course, we should never leave the subject of moronic advertising without touching briefly and gingerly, as one would handle a cockroach, on the strict formulaic creative approach so dear to package goods clients in the past. One of the most popular formulas relied on conflict resolution and is remembered, with disgust, as responsible for the rise of Aim Toothpaste in the 1970's. In this mini-drama, a child would be brushing his teeth when a nosy older relative would enter the bathroom uninvited and protest that the child should not be permitted to use a good-tasting toothpaste like Aim but should, instead, be tortured with a toothpaste that fights cavities and, presumably, tastes like sheep dip. At this point, the child's mother would storm into the bathroom and, scowling furiously at the elder family member, scream "Aim *has* fluoride! Aim *fights* cavities!" The fact that these nasty little dramas served to irritate the hell out of television viewers did not bother their creators because, they said, it sold toothpaste.

Rosser Reeves' stand against originality, and, some would say creativity, began by having a positive effect on advertising. But it boomeranged. Let me explain:

In the years after Claude Hopkins success, the agency business had become the exclusive domain of white males, mostly graduates of Ivy League schools and often the scions of wealthy Eastern Seaboard families. One, for example, was Chester Bowles, a founder of Benton and Bowles and a highly respected member of the Roosevelt and Truman administrations. His partner, Thomas Benton, became senator from Connecticut. These men produced lovely ads and posters using the best illustrators and touting the American Dream as if it had arrived for everyone. The ads reeked of a high-brow originality and creativity that oftentimes went right over the heads of the American public.

One of Reeves greatest contributions in advertising was to get the pretty fluff out of the way of the message. In doing so, he quoted Camus' *The Fall* (Reeves was, despite his rigid, anti-creative stance in advertising, a cultured gentlemen and poet with an enviable library).

Camus wrote, "How often, standing in the sidewalk involved in a passionate discussion with a friend, I lost the thread of the argument being developed because a devastating woman was crossing the street at that very moment."

Get the distractions out of your ads, no matter how pretty or original they may be, Reeves said, before they get in the way of your message. He called these distractions "vampire video." Unfortunately, this, one of his greatest contributions, is largely ignored today.

While Rosser Reeves' style of advertising was often effective, it treated the consumer like a tasteless moron, willing to swallow any claim, no matter how senseless or shallow, like an obedient sheep. As his message spread and more agencies began to imitate his style, the advertising industry turned itself into a joke, parodied and pilloried in books, radio, movies and television. And why not? It was nothing more than the American consumer striking back at an industry that seemed unable to hide or contain its contempt for him.

The man who saved advertising from itself.

Bill Bernbach, the creative genius behind the Doyle Dane Bernbach Advertising Agency, changed all that.

Bernbach was the man who brought civility, wit and, at the same time, egalitarianism to advertising. He was also largely responsible for bringing minorities and women—writers like Mary Wells Lawrence and Paula Greene—into the business. This infusion of fresh blood, plus Bernbach's insistence on talent and what he called "rigorous courtesy," revolutionized advertising every bit as much, if not more, than Reeves' stifling USP practicality.

Just as the public was beginning to consider advertising hopelessly imbecilic, Bernbach came along with ads that relied on grace, charm and wit to beguile consumers. It was not only a welcome change, it brought credibility back to the business.

There was a good reason Bernbach opened the agency business to minorities: as a Jew, he had been excluded at the beginning of his career.

Remember, this was a time when agencies were run and staffed, mostly, by WASPs, usually from the right schools and the right families. As a Jew with a public school education and a degree (B.A. in English) from NYU, he didn't fit in. Fortunately for Bernbach and the industry in general, there were a number of small Jewish agencies in New York City serving generally smaller Jewish clients. If you're interested in pursuing the subject, you'll find a wealth of information in Paula S. Rothenberg's work, *Race, Class and Gender in the United States*. Also, the short novel, *Focus*, by Arthur Miller gives a vivid and frightening picture of anti-semitism in the business world of New York in the 1930's, a picture that remained accurate through the 1940's and into the 1950's.

But Bernbach didn't start in the agency business, for reasons we can easily imagine. The future advertising pioneer began his first job in the mailroom of Schenley Industries for a whopping $16 a week. There, he spent his downtime creating ideas for ads for Schenley products. He was so proud of one that he sent it to the company's advertising agency, Lord and Thomas (the same Lord and Thomas once presided over by Albert Lasker and Claude Hopkins). He never heard back from the agency, but months later he did see his ad again, this time fully produced in a major publication.

Bernbach managed to retrieve his idea from a friend at Lord and Thomas and sent it, along with the published ad, to the management at Schenley. In a short time he was moved to the Marketing and Advertising Department where he caught the eye of the CEO, Grover Whalen. This association led to jobs writing political speeches as well as ads, so his skills of persuasion were not only honed but honed against the hard rock of New York's minority voting communities. He developed a talent for talking to people in their own terms, much as Hopkins had before him, but using warmth, humanity and—unusual for advertising at the time—humor.

In 1945, he went to work at a Jewish-owned agency, Grey Advertising (notice the lack of a Jewish name on the shingle) where he rose from copywriter to creative director in only four years. If this is getting boring, hold on; there's good reason for all of this Bernbach biography.

As the United States moved into the 1950's, we went from the tumult of worldwide depression and world war to an era of prosperity. People had seen enough history in the making; they wanted quiet lives in dull little communities where they could raise their families in peace and quiet. This was the age of Eisenhower, the age of conformity and McCarthyism. It's no wonder that the ideas of Rosser Reeves had such appeal. Artists and writers are bohemians and beatniks. Give me logical men with sound reasoning behind their work. Colleges began to produce MBA's, the industry's term for cocky young graduates with Masters in Business Administration degrees who had learned marketing and advertising from a textbook and were going to teach these old fogies on Madison Avenue a thing or two. With no background in the arts or humanities, they were natural disciples for the Rosser Reeves school of advertising.

In response to the onslaught of Reeves USP style and the impact of the new MBA's, Bernbach sent a memo to the management at Grey. I'm worried, he wrote, that we have begun to worship technique instead of substance. "Let us prove to the world that good taste, good art, good writing can be good selling." Implicit in this message was a deep respect for the sensibilities of the American people. Combined with his ear, and love for the common idiom, it produced a potent advertising punch.

With that, Bill Bernbach teamed with another Jew, Mac Dane, and an Irishman, Ned Doyle, to form one of the most storied advertising agencies of all time: Doyle Dane Bernbach. All that remains of it are a few initials on the title of a mega-agency, DDB Needham. I can't imagine that Bill Bernbach would be remotely comfortable there today.

Bernbach and his partners began an agency in which all you needed to succeed was talent and civility. He discouraged uniformity and dullness and encouraged innovation and fun. They started with Orbach's Department Store, a client that had followed its favorite copywriter from Grey. A few years later, a survey showed the wisdom of Ohrbach's move. New Yorkers were asked to rank order a list of department stores according to which spent the most money on advertising. Ohrbach's was listed third, behind Macy's and Gimble's. In fact, Ohrbach's was thirteenth in spending!

That kind of effectiveness quickly attracted another client, Levy's Jewish Rye Bread, a product that had always been marketed only to the city's large Jewish population. Bernbach recognized an opportunity. The agency produced posters, one featuring a smiling African-American boy with a once-bitten piece of rye bread in his hand, another with an Asian and still another with a Native American, all bearing the same copy line: "You don't have to be Jewish to love Levy's."

The results were phenomenal and attracted their first major clients, Polaroid and El Al Airlines, in 1954. Later, Doyle Dane Bernbach copy writer Paula Greene penned one of the most outstanding advertising lines ever written while working on Polaroid instant cameras:

"Even as the moment slips away, you can hold it in your hand."

In 1959, the agency landed the Volkswagen account. Suddenly we had a Jewish adman flogging a car created by Adolph Hitler. The result had to be exciting. And, of course, it was. The VW campaign was legendary and still occupies an important spot in advertising textbooks.

Eschewing the traditional car advertising of the time, VW was pro-moted as a small, strange-looking, perhaps even ugly, little car that was incredibly dependable and cheap to drive.

One ad pictured a VW Bug with the one-word headline, "Lemon." The copy explained that Volkswagens were so carefully inspected that even cars that would pass muster at most companies would be turned back into raw steel at VW. When the Moon Rover that astronauts drove around the surface of the moon was a subject of great interest, Bernbach put a picture of it in a VW ad with the headline, "it's ugly but it gets you there." Allegedly, when a research-driven critic criticized the "Lemon" ad, saying the 80 percent of the people looking through a newspaper did not read an ad's body copy, Bernbach predictably answered, "they read my body copy." Judging by the success of the VW campaign, they did indeed.

Why, despite Rosser Reeves well-founded objections to such clever originality, did Bernbach's work prove so wildly successful? Maybe the best answer came from Bernbach himself when he told a Reeves devotee who worked at Doyle Dane Bernbach, "You're right. All your facts are right. But you're still dull because you're saying everything that every-body else is saying."

When readers came upon a Bernbach ad, they were halted by its fresh-ness, honesty and, yes, Rosser, originality. They stayed with it, read it and got the message. But it's important to note that Bernbach also believed in the importance of focusing on a single, strong claim or concept.

Two giants, generally opposed to each other's style, had emerged. One had written a book that had crossed over the line between business and mainstream appeal. The other had evolved a look and feel to this work that made the consumer actually look forward to the next ad.

Meanwhile, David Ogilvy was watching, taking notes, and planning his own strategy.

Ogilvy weighs in.

Early in his new career, David Ogilvy discovered that he was a good writer and that he truly enjoyed writing. He was impressed by much of what Reeves offered, especially basing advertising on consumer research, but his writer's instinct rebelled at the brevity of text both Reeves and Bernbach insisted upon. Using his own research, plus a great deal from secondary sources, he initiated his own approach. Ogilvy admitted that only a small percentage of consumers would read past the headline and first paragraph of an ad. This small percentage, however, happened to be the same people who are most deeply interested in your product or service. In fact, once these readers had taken the time to read through the first few paragraphs, they generally continued to read the entire ad. Once you had the attention of this critical audience, Ogilvy reasoned, why stop short? Tell them everything!

As his hero, Claude Hopkins wrote, "Every ad, in my opinion, should tell a complete story. It should include every fact and argument found to be valuable."

What's more, Ogilvy declared, the pricier the product, the more people want to know about it, so write on. This last piece of information, however, did not keep him from writing paragraph after paragraph extolling the virtues of such common products as margarine. But, once again, he had found a way to differentiate his clients' ads from those of Ted Bates or Doyle Dane Bernbach.

As an interesting aside, Richard Pruitt, who worked for Ogilvy as a creative director in his Houston office, claims that his boss gave him quite a different version of how he came to create the format of his famous long-copy ads. According to Pruitt, Ogilvy told him he was looking at an ad written by Rosser Reeves and thinking about what he could do that would be entirely different yet just as effective or, hopefully, more so. He noted the large illustration hovering over a small block of copy. After a few minutes of study, he turned the ad upside down and then it struck him. He would have a large block of copy hovering over a small illustration. True story? Maybe, maybe not. But David Ogilvy had a typically British way of kidding himself and it does sound like a story he would have told to entertain his troops.

In addition to his long-copy approach, Ogilvy used readership studies from publications such as Time Magazine to add to the effectiveness of his ads. Time had learned, for example, that hurried readers might skip over a story but would stop to read the captions under the photographs. This, of course, led to the birth of Life Magazine, which was composed almost entirely of photos and captions. Ogilvy added captions to his ads, packing important selling messages into one of two boldface sentences beneath each photo. Also, he learned that magazines broke up their text with occasional small headlines to make it more attractive and readable. Looking at the long gray columns his long-copy approach dictated, he decided to do likewise, insisting that "crossheads" be inserted to make the lengthy message more inviting. Typically, he also insisted that these crossheads strongly reinforce the selling message.

Then, imitating his friend, Rosser Reeves, he published his first book, *Confessions of an Advertising Man,* spelling out what would come to be called the Ogilvy Way. Along with the methodology, an Ogilvy culture emerged that was, at once, as inclusive as Doyle Dane Bernbach but retained much of the clubiness of older, more traditional agencies. Men wore red suspenders and puffed on pipes in imitation of the master.

They talked about "Magic Lanterns" (slide shows) and "burrs of singularity" (charming and unusual turns of a phrase in copy). Many of these people were, frankly, butt-kissers. David Ogilvy's personality was of a type that he attracted what he dismissively called "toadies." In addition, he created within his company a new form of elitism similar to, if not worse than, that which existed pre-Bernbach.

Ogilvy worshipped Claude Hopkins and supplied a copy of *Scientific Advertising* to every employee. He wrote long, somewhat stylish copy, though what appeared stylish may simply have been a reflection of his never-fading Britishness. He railed against irrelevant and self-serving creative. And, to his great credit, he celebrated successful advertising from other agencies, like Doyle Dane Bernbach, that tended to break all of his rules.

David Ogilvy's rules, like Claude Hopkins, are sometimes rusty with age. But there is an overriding intelligence to them that bears attention.

Avoid celebrity spokespeople, he advises. The viewer remembers them and not your product.

Connect with honest emotion, but always give your viewer a rationale for her emotional decision.

Whenever appropriate, mention the product within the first 10 seconds of a commercial. Open strong and grab attention.

Show food in motion. Pour it, stir it. Make it come alive.

I love his negative opinion of jingles. How would you react, he asks, if you went to buy a refrigerator and the salesman started singing at you?

Music to set the mood and reinforce the message, however, can be valuable. Sound effects, like sausages sizzling in the pan, can be powerful.

Want to know more? If you are in the ad business and you haven't read *Ogilvy On Advertising*, you've cheated yourself and your client or company.

And so there were three living giants of advertising as the nation started to enter its most tumultuous decade since the Civil War, The Sixties.

IV

Love, Peace, Music and Advertising.

There's a mistaken belief that "The Sixties" exploded suddenly and from out of nowhere. Nothing could be further from the truth. The counter-culture that rose to the fore in one decade had deep roots in the preceding one. Figures of youthful rebelliousness like Elvis Presley and James Dean were products of the 1950's. Iconoclasts like Mort Sahl and Lord Buckley, writers like Jack Kerouac, intellectual giants like Marshall McLuhan (who published The Mechanical Bride, an inquiry into sex in advertising, in 1951), poets like Allen Ginsberg and jazz revolutionaries like Miles Davis arose in the 1950's. In a decade of stultifying conformity and McCarthyism-induced fear, these giants kept the American spirit of rebellion alive. There is a clear line from the Wobblies to Woody Guthrie to Pete Seeger to Bob Dylan. Love'em or hate'em, they gave breadth and meaning to the revolution that came to be The Sixties.

When did the revolutionary character of the Sixties first begin to emerge? You'll probably find a host of answers. To me, however, it began on February 2, 1960, when four courageous Black students from North Carolina A&T University sat down at the lunch counter in the F.W. Woolworth store of Greensboro, North Carolina. They had already proved that they were welcome to buy in the store, having purchased a few items before they sat down. Now they wanted to be welcome to eat there. They were not served that day, though they sat there until closing time. The following day, nine students showed up and took their places at the counter. They sat silently amid the taunts and flipped cigarette butts of angry whites. But they would not be turned away.

Within two weeks there were sit-in demonstrations, as they had come to be called, in 15 cities throughout the South. In New Haven the next month, 300 students from Yale University marched in support of the demonstrators. Wade-in demonstrations came to all-white beaches. Read-ins blocked the steps at all-white libraries. The dikes that had held back the legitimate demands of Black America were, after 200 years, beginning to crack.

The real change, however, was taking place in the living rooms and at the dining tables of Middle America. Young people, raised on World War II rhetoric about liberty, justice and brotherhood, were questioning their parents. White kids were asking how this country could justify the suppression of African-American rights. The answers they got were, to say the least, unsatisfactory. Black parents rarely did any better. Frightened by the violence their protests had met in the past, and anxious for the children's safety, they often advised caution. Small wonder the young people began to feel alienated from their parents' world.

On May 13 of 1960, another seminal event took place. Throughout the 1950's, alarmists had raised the flag of anti-communism so often and to such great effect that few dared oppose them. As part of this effort, a committee of Congress calling itself the House Committee on Un-American Activities came to San Francisco to hold hearings. They came to investigate anything they felt was "Un-American." When they turned their attention to a group of educators in the Bay Area, students from the University of California at Berkeley came to protest what they believed was an offense against the educators' rights as free citizens. You have to remember that, at the time, this group of congressmen considered themselves invulnerable, as they could point at any individual or group and destroy them with the single epithet, "Un-American."

The kids from Berkeley, however, didn't know enough to be afraid. To them, HUAC, as the committee was called, looked like a bunch of overly conservative, mean-spirited old men trying to throw their weight around. When the San Francisco Police, obviously horrified that anyone would protest against HUAC, tried to run the kids off, all hell broke loose. These were bright young people from prosperous families and they were not accustomed to being shoved by the police or anyone else when attempting to exercise their constitution rights. The cops shoved. The kids shoved back. Twelve people were injured in the ensuing riot and 52 were jailed. The Free Speech Movement was born and with it, Students for a Democratic Society and the New Left.

HUAC had managed the squelch the Old Left, reducing it by 1960 primarily to an odd group of eccentrics with no power and little appeal. But in their enthusiasm to stamp out every vestige of it, they played midwife to a New Left that was far more volatile and effective than anything they could imagine.

There was more.

In a small Asian nation named South Viet Nam, 200 members of the U.S. Army Special Forces had been assigned to assist and train the local armed forces who were under attack from a ragtag group of rebels known as the Viet Cong.

Not far from San Francisco, at the Veteran's Hospital in Menlo Park, a young writer named Ken Kesey had taken a part time job in the psychiatric ward where he was exposed to a mind-altering drug called LSD. He used the work experience in writing his first novel, *One Flew Over A*

Cuckoo's Nest. The LSD experience eventually led to Tom Wolfe's non-fiction novel, *The Electric Kool-Aid Acid Test*, which detailed the adventures of America's first band of itinerant hippies, Ken Kesey and the Merry Pranksters.

So as the Sixties got underway, these were the forces that were converging on America's television screens:

- A movement of young Black Americans willing to put their lives on the line in a non-violent struggle for social justice.
- A "gender gap" that would leave parents angry and frustrated with their children who marched under the banner, "don't trust anyone over 30."
- A movement of idealistic college students energized by ideals of American justice and in love with romantic notions about leftist revolution.
- The beginning of a troop deployment in Southeast Asia that would top out at over 500,000 and cost 50,000 American lives.
- A movement of drug-using young people enamored with Eastern religion and Utopian notions about a world ruled by love.

That was the serious side. As anyone who lived through or studied the decade can tell you, there was definitely a non-serious side as well. Indeed, after the uptight Fifties, the Sixties may have been the most fun since the Twenties. Attitudes relaxed. Television shows like the Smothers Brothers, Laugh-In and That Was The Week That Was poked fun at cherished institutions and had us laughing at ourselves.

Advertising, in the meantime, continued to divide news of earth-shattering change and iconoclastic humor with 60 and 30 second mini-dramas featuring women arguing over which detergent delivers the whitest white and cartoon characters cleaning floors. Obviously, something had to change.

How I washed up on the shores of advertising.

At this point, I want to introduce an advertising man who never had a major impact on the business. His one contribution to our learning here is that he stepped into the business, unprepared and naive, at this critical juncture in the nation's history. He did not come into the venerated hallways of Doyle Dane Bernbach or Ogilvy and Mather. Instead he began at a small advertising agency in the suburbs of Houston, Texas.

He is, of course, me.

In the early Sixties I was a newspaper reporter at the Houston Chronicle. My job was to edit the neighborhood news section which came out every Wednesday. For the most part, we covered garden clubs, PTA meetings, school boards and suburban town councils. Since I was the youngest, I was assigned the worst quarter of Houston, which included areas near the docks where there were no garden clubs or Rotary meetings. If you have ever heard boxer-turned-minister George Foreman talk about his youth on the mean streets of Northeast Houston, you've heard about my beat. I wouldn't be surprised to find that George and I had passed by each other on Lyons Avenue. It would be incorrect to say that I was one of the few whites who could be found in that part of town; I was the only white. But even I was rarely there after dark.

The U.S. military's publicity arm provided our neighborhood sections with an entire column every week by sending the latest news about boys from our areas. All four of us who edited a neighborhood section had devised an easy way to handle the military news; we arranged it into a special column with a standing headline such as "In Step" or "Passing Parade" or simply "Military News." Laying it out every week was a quick chore until I noticed that a young Black man from the area had been killed in this place called Viet Nam. I began to pull out the notices and set them aside. Before long, we were seeing several kids a month dying in a war I didn't pretend to understand.

So I read about Viet Nam. Later, I participated in a demonstration in front of President Lyndon Johnson's ranch. It was actually a poor excuse for a demonstration, but it got the attention of the managing editor of the Chronicle. He sternly admonished me that our job was to report the news, not make it.

That was Strike One.

Months later, I learned about a postal worker who spent his evening hours teaching Black kids the basics of getting a job; how to dress, how to write a resume, what to say. The basics. He came to my attention because he called his small organization Action for Youth and he got a small amount of outside financial support. This was important because President Johnson's Great Society included a program also called Action for Youth. Using federal money, Harris County Action for Youth was set up in a deserted supermarket next door to the Chronicle Building. They cleaned it up, brought in rows of desks, put typewriters on the desks and an earnest-looking person behind each desk. They typed reports and proposals and filed and collated. But I never saw them do a thing for the young people of Harris County. When they weren't busy with the typing and filing and collating, some of these earnest-looking people set about destroying the postal worker's small organization because, first, it was using an unregistered name that they, the professionals, now wanted, and, second, because, being a postal worker, he really didn't understand all the underlying dynamics affecting these children. All he did was help them get jobs.

Naturally, I published a story contrasting these two organizations. Strike two. The managing editor informed me that we were here to make friends, not enemies (definitely a pre-Watergate attitude) and besides I was attacking a program that was dear to the heart of President Johnson and President Johnson was dear to the heart of the Houston Chronicle.

Not long after that, a local minister called to complain that the neighborhood news section was becoming "too negative." I liked to think it was becoming relevant, a popular catchword of the times. Either way, it was strike three and I was out of there.

Before the managing editor could get around to firing me, I took a job covering local government for the Galveston News. It turned out to be a big mistake, since the News was even more anxious to make friends, particularly in the business community, than the Chronicle. After about a year or so of laying on the beach drinking beer and occasionally wandering by the sleepy city hall, I heard an interesting rumor. It was reported to me that the local brewery would, once a month, call the city's water treatment plant and tell them that they had just cleaned their barrels and the waste water was on the way. The people at the treatment plant would then shut a few doors and the waste water from the brewery would bypass the plant, going directly into Galveston Bay. A source at the plant confirmed the story. The detergents used at the brewery were so strong, he said, that it would wipe out all the bacteria in the treatment system, bacteria apparently being what cleaned the waste water. So they simply dumped it in the bay where it could kill the marine life instead.

I got plenty of backup and attribution. I turned the story in. It was killed. The editor already knew about it. And, I should have noticed, he was the president of the Galveston Chamber of Commerce. The editor/chamber president decreed that the truth would not be good for business. So it went untold.

When I got the news, the reporter sitting across from me, a guy named Ed Horn, said something that changed my life. He said, "if we're going to write public relations crap, we might as well get paid like PR writers." Two days later I was back in Houston looking for a writing job in public relations or advertising. Ed Horn, by the way, quickly found a much better-paying job writing PR for the Houston Port Authority.

Finding a job for which I had no qualifications.

My first stop was an agency called Goodwin, Dannenbaum Littman and Wingfield. The creative director looked at the book of clippings I had in hand and said he could tell nothing from them.

"Take this writing assignment," he said, handing me a packet. "It's for a brochure to announce a mortgage lending department at a bank. If you do a god job on it, I'll hire you."

I went right to the library and read as much as I could find on advertising, scanning *Confessions of an Advertising Man* in about three hours. Then I wrote, tore up and rewrote page after page until I felt I had described the function of mortgage lending and the bank's unique ability to perform it as well as it could be done. The next day, I returned with my copy to the creative director and proudly handed it to him. He read it, shaking his head sadly.

"This doesn't have the pizzazz we look for here at GDL&W," said. "Here, look at what I wrote."

He tossed me the copy he had written for the same brochure. The cover called for a cartoon and the headline read, "Ah Money, The Green Goddess of America." However, since I seemed like a nice guy, he sent me over to see the copy chief at another agency that was not as creative as his and therefore might accept a dullard like me. So I drove two blocks down Buffalo Speedway to Aylin Advertising Agency, where the copy chief once again looked at my samples, said he could tell nothing from them, handed me an assignment and said if he liked what I came up with, he would hire me.

I wasn't going to fall for that one again. The assignment was to write a television commercial for Gulf States Utilities, an electric utility in East Texas and Louisiana, touting the dependability and low cost of their electricity. I knew that Gulf States supplied electricity to Huntsville, Texas, where the state penitentiary was located. Back then, Texas still operated Old Sparky, its infamous electric chair, right there in Huntsville.

So in my commercial, a convict on death row is being led to the chair. The priest asks him if he has anything to say before he goes. Yes, the prisoner answers, I just want to say I'm proud that it'll cost 12 percent less for me to ride the lightning than it did for my uncle, Crazy Earl, back in 51. And the service is so dependable now, you can anticipate no unseemly interruptions. By now, they have reached Old Sparky and our convict is strapped in. The priest wipes a tear from his eye and says, "good-bye Louie…and more power to you." We then cut to an overhead shot of the town as the lights dim and the logo comes up full screen.

"This is terrific!" the copy chief said. "You're hired!"

"Great," I said. "When do we propose it to the client?"

"Oh, we could never show him this," the copy chief said. "He would fire our agency."

And so I fell down the rabbit hole of advertising, never to return.

Winning gold.

I had indeed ended up in Wonderland. Less than a year after I started work at Aylin Advertising, the copy chief quit and left me with the job. About the same time, the boss, Robert Aylin, attended a seminar in which he learned that no agency could consider itself truly professional unless it had a young, hip creative director. Aylin didn't have one of those, but he did have me and I certainly looked the part. So now, only slightly more qualified than when I first walked in the door, I was an official creative director. Being a reporter by nature, I set about finding out what a creative director does. One of the things I discovered was the Award Show.

Award Shows are when the people of advertising dress up and gather in a hotel ballroom where they eat, drink incredible amounts of alcohol and congratulate each other over the work they've done during the past year. Careers are made at Award Shows. Accounts are lost and gained. Fist fights break out. It's probably the most fun you can have outside a theme park.

The most important show in Texas at the time was the Dallas Society of Visual Communications Annual Show. I determined to do well there and, in doing so, put Aylin on the creative map. In addition, it was the first show in Texas to award a gold medal for the best copy in the show.

I had a magazine campaign for an air cargo company that I felt was a sure winner. My secretary also convinced me to enter a radio commercial for a local Volkswagen dealer that she especially liked, even though I didn't think it had a chance.

The air cargo campaign won an award of merit and hung outside the ballroom along with hundreds of other ads. The VW dealership commercial won Gold for best copy.

Go figure.

We introduce bank credit cards.

Even small agencies get some exciting chores. Our client, Bank of the Southwest, became the first Houston bank to offer a credit card. Back then it was called BankAmericard. It's long since changed to Visa. We introduced that card with full page newspaper ads that I wrote to meet the demands of every Hopkins-Reeves-Ogilvy rule at my command. The results were quite good, but that may have been because the cards were mailed out all over the area. We started in the fall and by the holiday season the bank was almost overwhelmed by demand. The bank's marketing vice president decided that we needed a Christmas commercial but, he told me, they didn't want anything that worked too well.

As a result, I produced a whimsical animated commercial in the style of Peter Max in which an evil South Pole Elf steals all of Santa's presents. Later he undergoes a change of heart and wants to undo his evil deeds. Santa tells him it's too late, but the South Pole Elf says no, and produces a BankAmericard with which he purchases all the needed toys and pays them off monthly at a high rate of interest, which we failed to mention. Just in case this story sounds a little familiar, please know that the commercial was produced in 1969, two years before *How The Grinch Stole Christmas* was published.

The commercial that broke all the rules and wasn't intended to draw much business produced a landslide of BankAmericard business. All of which proves that, on the rare occasion that you have a product or service that people really want, just about any reasonably informative ad will do.

It also won the Gold Medal for best commercial at the Houston Art Directors Show. And why not? Psychedelic faux Peter Max, young writer changing the image of a crusty old bank. This was no white tornado or toilet-cleaning genie. This was a love-is-all-you-need, flower power, groovy hip commercial.

As a result, early in my career I developed a jaundiced view of Award Shows. Not that I stopped entering them. But I learned not to be too elated if I won something or disappointed if I didn't.

We'll get back to Award Shows later.

I stayed with Bob Aylin for four years and learned more than I thought I had at the time. Bob was a promoter by nature and it was a joy to be around his energy. He also taught me one of the most important lessons I learned about writing advertising and I don't know if he made it up or read it somewhere. So if I fail to give proper credit here, I apologize.

The lesson was AIDA. Easy to remember because of the opera. It meant:
Attention
Interest
Desire
Action

And it was Bob's only formula for writing a commercial. Get their Attention (open dramatically), engage their Interest (involve them in the product), create Desire (make them hot for it) and call for Action (tell them what you want them to do).

You'd be surprised how many commercials I've seen fail over the years simply because the advertiser didn't tell the audience what he or she wanted them to do. It doesn't have to be a hammer-handed, overly explicit call to action. But it should at least be strongly implied. Buy this product. Call this number. Come by today.

By 1968, advertising agency creative departments were overrun with the tragically hip; bearded and long-haired young people who considered themselves potentially great writers and artists who had become trapped in the mundane world of advertising. I joined them enthusiastically. But I had a major fault: I was actually interested in the success of the agency's clients and I had reservations about the television-driven excesses of our business. Some others tolerated this in me, others didn't. One who thought like I did was Don Bellisario, a creative director at the Bloom Agency in Dallas. He hired me for $2,000 a year *less* than I was making at Aylin. But he promised me experience on major regional and national accounts. And he made good on his promise.

Don, by the way, is one of those rare individuals who has an instinctive sense of what the average American will respond to, rather than what would appeal to our fellow creative people. Unfortunately for our business, he left and went on to produce some of the best adventure shows on television, including Magnum P.I., Quantum Leap and JAG.

The Bloom Agency was, like Doyle Dane Bernbach in New York City, a unique place in time. Run by a retired manager of advertising for a

Dallas newspaper named Sam Bloom, it was an adventurous, creative agency that was genuinely fun to work for. The reason started at the top. Sam Bloom was one of the kindest and most supportive bosses anyone could have. As I joined it, however, it was beginning to change. Sam's son, Bob Bloom, did not share his father's easy-going style. Bob wanted to change it from a creative boutique to a hard-driving package goods agency. While the change was causing a lot of political damage, it exposed me to two very important points of view.

Let me summarize some of the learning and deliver on a couple of the money-saving tips I promised.

TIP 1: Avoid New Product Euphoria

Bob Bloom's first big hit in the packaged goods category was Riviana Foods out of Houston. Doesn't ring a bell? I can tell you why. Riviana was a combination of two rice giants, River Brand and Carolina, who had purchased Mahatma Rice, Austex Chili, Hill's Dog Food and, believe it or not, a line of Kosher foods. Like all of the new conglomerates of the age, they were aggressive about new products. Legends could be made, heroes recognized, in the new products department.

The first one they brought us was a rice dish similar to Golden Grains venerable Rice-A-Roni except that, instead of the dangerous business of adding cold water to a hot pan, the water would be added to the rice mix in advance, sealed and baked in the oven.

We tested the product in focus groups. I came up with a list of names. Bake-It-Easy was the runaway winner. We came up with and tested several commercials. The winner was one I had written in which a talking oven begs the housewife to let him cook prepare the rice dish. It scored high. The client was effusive. The agency was delirious. But the consumer was unmoved. The demand for new rice dishes was not high; most people were okay with what they had. It didn't meet projections.

What happened? The same thing that happens to thousands of new products every year; the agency and client caught new-product euphoria. Everyone deeply wanted success for the product and managed to put the brightest spin on every new development. Bake-It-Easy should have been tanked before it was ever tested.

Before you go to the huge expense of introducing a new product, make sure you are not caught up in the euphoria. Ask the tough questions. Don't throw good money after bad. And take everything your agency says with a grain of salt. They desperately want its success because they are staring at a significant increase in income. Is there a real need in the market? Does your new product offer a discernible and attractive difference? If not, tank it now.

TIP 2: Let your consumer drive your business. Then reflect it in your advertising.

One of the best things Don Bellisario did for me was to put me on the Southwest Airlines account and give me plenty of freedom to work directly with the president of the airline, Lamar Muse. At its startup, Southwest had three Boeing 737 Jets serving three cities: Houston, Dallas and San Antonio. To call it an "airline" seemed an exaggeration. It had been created because the airlines serving these markets, Braniff and Texas International, were doing a terrible job. They were far too interested in developing major national and international business to devote much attention to intrastate service in their own home state. According to the legend, Lamar, Herb Kelleher, a San Antonio lawyer, and Rollin King, an airline pilot, first drew up the plan for Southwest

Airlines on a cocktail napkin. Seems appropriate to the times.

They brought their idea to Sam Bloom and he pulled in his creative staff. Fortunately, the lead copy writer, a guy from Cleveland named Don Smetna, was deathly afraid of flying. He coined the slogan, "The Somebody Else Up There Who Loves You," taking off on the popular Rocky Grazziano biopic, starring Paul Newman, "Somebody Up There Loves Me."

"Love" was a very popular word in those days. We still had "Flower Children," the "Love Generation" and "Make Love, Not War" rattling around in our collective consciousness. So the idea of us, the airline, loving them, the passenger, seemed very hip. We named the drinks "Love Potions," a free seat in case you ever encountered a full flight became "The Love Seat," and the Boeing 737's were christened "Love Birds." All of this love would be delivered in the form of exceptional, though thoroughly informal, service.

The Love theme was fortuitous in ways we didn't even consider at the time. There were three forces loose in the youth culture of the time that were attracting a great deal of attention. There was a civil rights movement, an anti-war movement and the hippie movement, which centered around love in its many forms. Neither civil rights nor anti-war slogans translated into particularly motivating sales messages. But love, ah love, that we could use. Not that we were the only people to do it. Wells Rich Greene was flogging a line of Love Cosmetics for adolescents. Coca Cola gathered young people from all over the world on a hilltop in Italy to sing, "I'd like to teach the world to sing in perfect harmony...I'd like to buy the world a Coke..." But our version of Love was neither cloying or adolescent.

If any group of people in the world deserved a little more love back then it was the airline passengers traveling between Houston, Dallas and San Antonio. They spent inordinate amounts of time waiting in departure lounges, staring out the window at warm, sunny skies while hearing that their flight was delayed because of weather in Chicago or New York. When the airplane finally arrived, it was staffed by a bunch of short-tempered flight attendants who had been dealing with angry passengers all day. It was no fun and a lot of them, if they had the time, would opt to drive.

Southwest came along with an affordable fare and flights that were almost always on time because they never went north of Amarillo and were rarely full. The drinks were free, the flight attendants were cheerful and they always seemed to arrive a few minutes ahead of schedule.

It clearly set Southwest Airlines apart from the other carriers of the time, especially Braniff, its major competitor. Braniff was heavily into sophistication, with cappuccinos following meals and flight attendants who went through fashion changes during the flight. Braniff's agency, Wells Rich Greene, made you feel that, in flying Braniff, you were a member of an exclusive club. In fact, most of the major airlines of the time thought highly of themselves. Eastern Airlines proclaimed itself "The Wings of Man" in a series of beautiful and incredibly self-serving commercials. A small carrier, Allegheny Airlines, later spoofed Eastern with an ad in which they proclaimed themselves "The Wings of Sam," showing a harried salesman named Sam who just wanted affordable, on-time flights, forget the fashion shows.

Southwest took the same tack, only with a more positive spin than "The Wings of Sam." We were the airline that offered love and attention, that got you there on time for only $26, the price of any ticket between our three cities at the time. We presented Southwest as a fun airline to fly. Flight attendants wore shorts and knit tops, the drinks were free and the flight announcements were informal and chatty.

An important point: Lamar Muse brought the attitude of the advertising into the flight itself, urging the flight attendants to adopt the casual, fun attitude of the commercials. And the commercials reflected a fun, looser attitude in the culture. The flight attendants proved so good at it that we produced a new set of commercials featuring flight attendants delivering the pitch. That produced added credibility when the passengers found themselves greeted by someone who they had seen on television the night before. Esquire Magazine produced an issue on "The Best of Everything." The cover photograph was of a Southwest Airlines flight attendant. Our little three-airplane operations now boasted the world's best fight attendants.

People saw the advertising and experienced the flights and said, "these people are honestly delivering on what they promise, and it's something I want."

It was as if the arising culture of love, informality and fun had given birth to an airline. And Southwest's size, in this light, became an advantage rather than a disadvantage.

Of course, Braniff did not take this lying down. They countered by cutting their fare to $13 in all three of Southwest's markets. If we met the fare, Muse said, it would bankrupt Southwest.

That day, Ray Trapp, the very capable account supervisor on the business, appeared at my cubicle looking ashen. Muse had written an ad attacking Braniff and its tactics and wanted to run it, full-page, in all the major newspapers of Dallas, Houston and San Antonio. He handed me Muse's copy. It was not only inflammatory, it violated everything we had been trying to do in establishing Southwest's personality. Trapp asked me if I could rewrite it and tone it down but still keep it hot enough to satisfy Muse. I worked all day on it, sending version after version to Lamar, who kept making it stronger and sending it back. This continued until nightfall when Herb Kelleher, the attorney and co-founder of the airline arrived. That night, we all sat around the marble table in Sam Bloom's conference room and literally negotiated our way through the copy. Kelleher granted me my headline: "Nobody's Going To Shoot Us Out Of The Sky For A Lousy $13!"

We worked through the body copy with Muse making a statement he felt should be included, then Kelleher countering that the statement was potentially libelous. They would stare at each other while I scribbled away. Kelleher had shown up at the meeting with a terrible cold made worse by the flight, so he was in no mood to be trifled with. Muse, on the other hand, was a gruff, headstrong person who could be difficult even under the best of circumstances. I was seated between them and, as the writer, was expected to find some sort of compromise to satisfy them both. Fortunately, I was able to, time after time. About three-quarters of the way through the evening, Kelleher smiled at me and said, "you would have made a hell of a lawyer." At the time, that was considered a compliment. Morgan Ziller, a superb designer and art director, did the layout and made sure it got to the newspapers on time. The message was that a uncaring Goliath, Braniff, was trying to kill a David, Southwest, that had brought low fares and dependable service to the skies of Texas. If you demand a $13 fare, the ad said, we will give it you. But if you willingly pay the $26 fare, you will help keep our airline flying and earn our gratitude. Seems like a dubious proposition, but…well, read on.

The next day we joined employees of the airline on the streets of downtown Dallas handing out copies of the ad. People began to show up at the gates just to see what was happening. To a hard-headed pragmatist like Lamar Muse, "gratitude" was a foggy promise. He wanted to offer something more tangible and he proposed a choice between a fifth of Jack Daniels and a fifth of Johnny Walker.

"What about people who don't drink?" he was asked.

Lamar look puzzled, apparently unfamiliar with the concept of non-drinking. "Well," he answered, "give them an ice bucket."

And that's what we did. If a passenger said he wanted to pay full fare, he was immediately given his choice between with bottle of whiskey or an ice bucket. The word spread quickly, and since most of our passengers were business people traveling on an expense account, a $13 difference would be of little import, and a free bottle of whiskey would be nice to take home. For the first time in Southwest's short history, our flights were full and our future was assured. Richie Schiera, a fellow writer on the account, and I went down to the Braniff gate at Love Field and thanked them. They had, in their animosity, saved our account and Lamar's airline.

TIP 3: *Find innovative ways to make your positioning pay off.*

One day, Lamar Muse called me to his office to answer a question that could have been answered on the phone. But when Muse wanted to discuss something important, he did it face to face.

"I'm thinking about re-opening Hobby Airport in Houston. I know you're from Houston so I wanted to get your opinion."

"Why in the world," I asked, "would you want to do that?"

"Because," he said, "it's only three miles from downtown. It's much more convenient."

Don't do it, I advised him. I had recently been to Hobby and it was in shambles. Hobby International had been Houston's only airport once but was now seriously neglected, I told him. Lamar was disappointed. He had called me in because he thought that, what with my long hair and beard, beads and neo-hippie clothing, I would be in favor of his radical idea.

Of course, he went ahead and opened Hobby. Within a few years it was handling more arrivals and departures than it had when it was Houston's only airport, and every one of them was a Southwest Airlines flight.

Lamar Muse, in his pragmatic manner, had given "Love" new meaning; we love our passengers, therefore we provide them with low fares, frequent flights and, now, close-in airports. In time, the free drinks would disappear, along with the sexy shorts and knit tops. But the combination of low fares, frequent flights and close-in airports drove Southwest from the little, three-airplane, three-destination carrier one of the 10 largest airlines in America.

Braniff, on the other hand, went into bankruptcy, struggled to recover, and failed, never to be seen again.

In 1981, Tim McClure of GSD&M changed the "love" in Southwest's mission to "spirit." But it not change the way the airline thinks or operates.

V

The Amazing Mr. Kelleher

At some point, after I had left the Bloom Agency, a mistake I still regret, Southwest's management underwent a wrenching change. Herb Kelleher and Rollin King pushed Lamar Muse out, for reasons that I can fully understand, given Muse's abrasive personality. They hired a man named Howard Putnam to replace Muse. Putnam, making a mistake even worse than I had made in leaving Bloom, later jumped the Southwest ship and went down with Braniff. So Kelleher took over the top job himself. To this date, Herb Kelleher remains CEO of Southwest Airlines. There is no president. He does, however, have a second-in-command named Colleen Barrett. Ms. Barrett has, over the years, upheld the tradition of "LUV," as she prefers it. Herb, as everyone at the airline calls him, has proved to be one of America's most respected business leaders. What he has done best is to hew closely to the original position established in 1970. He hands out drinks and peanuts on flights, engaging his customers in conversation. He takes over bar tending duties at company functions. And he may show up for a flight inexplicably dressed as Elvis.

Southwest employees are no less extroverted. I believe it all started the first year Southwest was in operation. A flight attendant named Debbie Hairstrom was upset over having to work on Easter Sunday. There was nothing to be done, she was told. Southwest operated on a shoestring budget and there was no allowances for extra days off. Showing the true Southwest spirit, Debbie showed up for work that Sunday, smiling and happy. She was wearing an Easter Bunny costume and she worked every flight in it. Since then, flight attendants and gate personnel have shown up in all sorts of costumes. And that's not all. They have sung the flight information to the tune of the Beverly Hillbillies theme song, recited poetry and made up games to entertain the passengers.

Herb tells his people, "we take our customers seriously, but we never take ourselves seriously."

He also enjoys intense devotion, verging on adoration, from many of his employees. The reason is simple: Herb Kelleher believes the success of Southwest Airlines is dependent on its people. Sure, lots of CEO's talk that talk but Herb Kelleher is the only one I've seen walk the walk. He genuinely cares about the people he works with, and it shows.

A simple example. One day a small film crew came to shoot and record an interview with Kelleher. He apologized but said he could only spare 15 minutes. However, before doing the interview, he introduced himself to, and shook hands with, every member of the crew. After the interview, he took the time to thank each crew member individually, calling each one by name. It wasn't a trick he learned in a memory class; it's vintage Kelleher. There's not another like him.

No other airline delivers the value that Southwest offers on a routine basis. No other airline can match Southwest's profit performance over the years it has been in service. And it all began with a powerful and unique positioning backed up by a dedicated and courageous management.

Listen to what Herb Kelleher has to say (excepted from the book, *Leader to Leader*):

"Our real accomplishment is to have inspired our people to buy into a concept, to share a feeling and an attitude, to identify with the company—and then to execute."

When Southwest opened its California markets, many of us worried that the culture would not extend that far. We were wrong because we thought a company's culture was something the company imposed upon it's people. In fact, Southwest's culture seduced these new people until they carried it with the fervor of the converted.

"But you need to spend more time on the intangibles than the tangibles to create that kind of buy-in... We are not afraid to talk to our people with emotion. We're not afraid to tell them, 'We love you.' Because we do."

Kelleher has never been afraid to show emotion. During filming of a commercial for Ronald McDonald House, Southwest's favorite charity, he let tears run down his cheeks as he talked on camera. "Not you basic hard-boiled airline executive," director Jeb Schary commented.

"One of the managers of our People Department once said, 'The important thing is to take the bricklayer and make him understand that he is building a home, not just laying bricks.' So we take the building a home approach. This is what you're doing not only for yourself but for society; giving people who otherwise would not be able to travel the opportunity to do so; making it possible for grandparents to see their grandchildren for the holidays, or for a working Mom to take her son to see the World Series."

It's equally important to make sure the copywriter, the media buyer and everyone else know that they're not just laying bricks.

"A financial analyst once asked me if I was afraid of losing control of our organization. I told him I'd never had control and I never wanted it. If you create an environment where the people truly participate, you don't need control. They'll know what needs to be done and they'll do it. And the more that people will devote themselves to your cause on a voluntary basis, a willing basis, the fewer hierarchs and control mechanisms you need."

This is also known as getting the best out of your people.

"With deregulation, that market strategy (a low cost, high frequency point-to-point operation) was in question. We could have brought in 747's and flown non-stop from New York to Los Angeles. It was a defining moment…(after consulting people throughout the company) we decided not to go head-to-head with the international carriers, but to build on the strategy that had worked so well in the past."

Legendary Texas football coach Darrell Royal, when asked if he were going to change his team's style of play before a big bowl game, answered that he believed in "dancing with the one that brung us." Nobody needed another coast-to-coast airline with 747's. But there was a demonstrated need for what Southwest offered all over the country. So much so, in fact, that various city governments have made presentations to Southwest's management in hopes of enticing then to fly into their airport.

"My best lesson in leadership came during my early years as a trial lawyer. Wanting to learn from the best, I went to see two of the most renowned litigators in San Antonio try cases. One sat there and never objected to anything, but was very gentle with witnesses and established *a rapport with the jury. The other was an aggressive, thundering hell-raiser. And both seemed to win every case. That's when I realized there are many different paths, not one right path. That's true of leadership as well. People with different personalities, different approaches, different values succeed not because one set of values is superior, but because their values and their practices are genuine. And when you and your organization are true to yourselves—when you deliver results and a singular experience—customers can spot it from 30,000 feet."*

The people at Southwest aren't afraid to be themselves. That's why they invent on-flight contests and singalong announcements, both of which contribute to that singular experience.

"Fifteen years ago, competitors were saying, "We're going to be the next Southwest Airlines. But they didn't really understand who we were. Most of them did not really imitate Southwest Airlines; they just ended up creating new versions of themselves."

Roy Spence, president of Southwest's advertising agency, GSD&M, echoed this in an address to his staff. "If we try to be like other advertising agencies, we'll only end up being a worse them. Instead let's become a better us." Great advice for any company in any industry.

What does all this have to do with getting more for your advertising dollar? Just this: the people who work on the Southwest Airlines account adopt the enthusiasm and drive of the people they are working with. An account manager once commented on the enthusiasm of the Southwest staff, after working on a cross promotion between his client and Southwest Airlines, "they flat wore me out."

They are enthusiastic because they are loved. And they know it because there has never been a layoff in the history of Southwest Airlines.

In turn, their devotion to their client is translated into the best airline advertising in the country.

Want more effective advertising? Become a more genuine company. That won't be easy, you may say. But no one ever said it would be, did they?

VI

Positioning And The Big Idea.

Television began in the late 1940's but its full effect didn't appear until the early 1960's when children raised on it began to reach maturity. A strong clue to its effect is contained in Marshall McLuhan's *The Gutenberg Galaxy* and *Understanding Media*. Print, McLuhan maintained, expelled humankind from tribalism, when people gathered in groups to hear and share stories, into a cold world in which he sat alone and silent. Print made us linear, so that we thought in a linear mode and organized and understood things along straight lines. Television changed all that, returning us to a new form of tribalism and a growing global village.

What this meant was that the young people raised on television did not think the way their parents did, and vice versa. They could absorb more visual and audible information at a faster rate. What could look and feel like chaos to a linear thinker might make perfect sense to this new generation.

Hopkins, Reeves and Ogilvy were linear. Bernbach was a bridge between linear and non-linear because the non-linear wanted beauty, taste and emotion along with its serving of rational information.

Of course, there no such thing as a linear or non-linear thinker. We all do some of both. But there was a difference in the way the two generations thought and McLuhan's explanation made some degree of sense.

Equally upsetting to all the old rules was the world that presented itself outside our front door. In 1959, Clark Kerr, President of the University of California, said of his students, "The employers will love this generation. They are going to be easy to handle."

A year later that easy-to-handle generation was shutting down his campus and rioting in the streets of San Francisco.

In August of 1964, a Black neighborhood of Watts in Los Angeles exploded in a riot. Two years later, it was Cleveland, then Chicago. The riots spread across the country as the 12 percent of Americans of African descent made it clear that they would, in the words of Mexican revolutionary Emiliano Zapata, rather die on their feet than live on their knees. Imagine the middle American white emerging from the complacent Fifties to hear Black activist H. Rap Brown proclaim, "The white man don't want nothing Black but a Cadillac. We must wage guerrilla war on these honkies!"

The Johnson administration's attempts to appear in control were futile. The President's press secretary, Bill Moyers, threw up his hands in saying, "The credibility gap is getting so big we can't even believe our own leaks."

Credibility was getting harder and harder to come by. If the President of the United States was having a hard time establishing any what was an advertising agency supposed to do?

Advertising people broke into camps. On one side there were those who clung to the teachings of Hopkins, Reeves and Ogilvy. They came to be identified as marketing-oriented. On the other were those searching for new ways to influence consumers. They were known as creative-driven. As you might imagine, the marketing-oriented folks were more linear in their thinking, the creative-driven more non-linear. Marketing-oriented people pointed to the formula success of Proctor and Gamble's advertising. The creative-driven pointed out that P&G's commercials had so much media weight, ie. ran so often, that they could not be ignored and therefore had to be successful. A truly creative commercial, however, broke through the clutter more quickly and offered, in the terminology of the trade, "more bang for the buck."

It was this latter argument that began to turn the heads of American businessmen. They could tolerate this new type of advertising person, with the long hair and funny clothes, if he or she could produce commercials that actually worked harder.

Creative hot shops like Jack Tinker and Partners and Doyle Dane Bernbach began to attract more attention. More established agencies fought back by hiring away their most creative people. A friend at Doyle Dane Bernbach at the time told me that their offices were old and musty and had no air conditioning. Their writers and art directors would be hired away at much larger salaries by old-guard agencies who wowed them with plush offices and luxurious amenities. Within six months they would be back at Doyle Dane Bernbach, asking for their old jobs back. More often than not, I was told, they were rehired at their old salary. And they were glad to be back. A bigger problem for the creative shops was the entrepreneurial spirit. Paula Greene left to form her own agency. So did Mary Wells Lawrence and George Lois and a host of other creative luminaries.

With the older recipes for success being pushed aside, except of course at the agencies that were built on them, advertising people began to look for new and better theories on which to base their work and, equally important, explain it to their clients. The two that emerged weren't so much new concepts as recognition of the way advertising had evolved. They were also, very often, part and parcel of each other.

Something remarkable was happening in the world and in the advertising business. One example in which it was clearly evident was the new campaign for Pepsi-Cola. Pepsi had, over the years, gone from a value story, "12 big ounces, that's a lot," to a peer group approval story, "be sociable, drink Pepsi, be up to date with Pepsi." It was well-known that soda pop appealed to a young audience. Young people were, as stated earlier, going through various forms of rebellion. What was common to them all was a quest for individuality and experience. Pepsi's agency, an old guard company named BBDO, took advantage of it. They created a campaign that identified Pepsi as the soft drink of the young, independent seeker of life's experiences, leaving Coca-Cola as the soft drink of grumpy old people.

The theme of the campaign was, "you've got a lot to live and Pepsi's got a lot to give." As with previous Pepsi campaigns, it was made into a jingle, or song. When Spencer Michelin told me he had written the song, I asked him what that line meant. He just smiled and shrugged. Still, the images used in the campaign were unusual for commercials. They concentrated on people who looked real and situations that looked natural. The casting was to the edge of the envelope.

Here's the interesting thing: this campaign—with a theme line that was sung anthem-like with a rising chorus despite not making much sense—was a huge hit with the youth market. They identified with it. With the young man in hiking gear striding boldly across a suspension bridge somewhere the wilderness of whatever. With the young people in love. With the independence. Yes, they said, I have a lot to live and...what? Pepsi has a lot to give...well, okay, Pepsi it is.

I believe that was a seminal campaign in modern advertising. Certainly there were imitators that followed. In fact, the jingle industry was overwhelmed for the next several years. But few others captured the non-linear fusion of music, picture and theme that defied logic but spoke volumes to its audience. At the same time, it broke every rule we've discussed. There is no Unique Selling Proposition here. It is beautiful. Artful. Horrors, Mr. Ogilvy, it's a song!

Whether they knew it or not at the time, the creative people at BBDO had *positioned* Pepsi-Cola. They had given it a position, a place in the market as well as their target audience, that was entirely its own. They didn't try to make Pepsi the preferred drink of everyone everywhere. Just young people. Beyond that, just hip young people with a desire for life's experiences. Never mind that their experience-seeking may never go beyond daydreams in their room.

Advertising creative people also broke rules when they discovered the consumer had a sense of humor. Wells Rich Greene took the new Benson and Hedges 100 millimeter cigarette, somewhat longer than the normal cigarette of the times, and showed all its disadvantages. They showed it getting caught in elevator doors, bumping into walls and getting accidentally clipped off. It was not the first cigarette of this length, but it was certainly the only one people noticed. Imagine, in the context of Reeves and Ogilvy, advertising the disadvantages of your product and still managing to make it look fun and sophisticated. Did it work? You bet it did.

Of course, This was not the first time positioning had been used, though I don't think anyone called it that at the time. Doyle Dane Bernbach, for example, had done it brilliantly with Volkswagen.

The VW Beetle was positioned for young people who needed a cheap car that ran on fumes, people who also had enough chutzpah to pass on that dumb-looking, bottom-of-the-line Chevy in favor of a truly ugly car. It was fun and practical, both. But you had to have the nerve to be seen in a car that had a trunk in front, the engine in back. no radiator and looked like it didn't know if it was coming or going. Years before, the Kaiser company had offered a small car called the Henry J, boasting of it's good looks and fuel economy and appealing to just about everyone who drove. It bombed. Maybe if they'd made it funnier looking and limited its appeal to the young and adventurous, it might have survived.

Doyle Dane Bernbach also produced a classic in positioning for Avis Rent-A-Car. The campaign was conceived by Paula Greene, copy chief at DDB at the time. The proposition was, "we're number two. We try harder. We have to." Bill Bernbach claims that he did not like the campaign but Greene was so enthusiastic about it that he let her present it. The chairman of Avis at the time, Robert Townsend (author of *Up The Organization* and *Further Up The Organization*) was just enough of a corporate iconoclast to give it a try. It was wildly successful because, first, it was brilliant positioning, and, two, because it, like the Southwest Airlines advertising before it, was a double-edged sword. It motivated both the customer and the Avis employee. Before long, Avis people really were trying harder and customers really were feeling better served. They positioned the company and the employees followed.

The term, "positioning," began to show up in articles and agency pitches. But it meant different things to different people. Basically, it means to find a unique place for your product to reside within the consumers mind, as opposed to a unique selling proposition. Look at the Volkswagen advertising from the early Sixties for an excellent example. Consider 7-Up repositioning itself as "The UnCola." Or Southwest Airlines' repositioning in the Eighties as "The Company Plane," an airline so convenient you could substitute it for your corporate jet.

To many, however, positioning evolved into a form of niche marketing; find a small subset of the population and market your product directly to them. It sounds like either a dumb move or a desperate attempt to survive, but it has often proved to be quite effective. It often succeeds because the enthusiasm it received within the niche market halos out. The product becomes "cool." This has been especially effective in beer and wine marketing. In fact, it has reached the point that no one wants to be seen drinking a beer with a major label.

To others, it was a response to an over-communicated society. An example of this position on positioning can be found in a book with the unwieldy title, *Positioning, The Battle For Your Mind. How To Be Seen And Heard In The Overcrowded Marketplace* by Al Ries and Jack Trout. By the time it was published in 1981, clutter was a far bigger problem than when Claude Hopkins first encountered at the turn of the century. Ries and Trout used this fact as a springboard to discuss the need for at least an appearance of uniqueness in the presentation of the product. A lot of it, however, harks back to problems Hopkins dealt with 80 years earlier.

First, the consumer is not interested in hearing about your product nor does he or she care how proud you are of it. The consumer wants to know what your product can do for her, and only what your product can do for her. I call this getting on the consumer's side of the net. The fact is, most consumers look at their relationship with the manufacturers of the products they use as adversarial. All they want is my money, they think, and if the product doesn't perform properly, I'm going to have a hard time getting my money back. At the same time, consumers yearn for a brand or name they can be loyal to. Unfortunately, we don't offer them many opportunities. How loyal can you be to an airline that bumps you at the end of a trying day, or shortens the distance between seats until you have to fly in agony for several hours while flight attendants either ignore you or treat you with disdain? A senior flight attendant with one of America's premier international airlines once told me, "hey, pal, all you bought was a ticket."

In other words, forget all the service implied in our commercials, all you get is a seat from here to there. What made this statement most telling, by the way, is that the flight attendant who said it works only in first class!

How loyal will you be to a company whose 800 number bounces you around between recorded messages that usually return you to where you started without yielding a single answer? Or web sites with no easily accessible system for communicating with the company and expecting a prompt response?

Today, affordable technology exists that allows customers to communicate on-line with a live operator, one who they can see speaking to them on their computer screen. Yet very few companies avail themselves of it. That's dumb.

A century ago, Claude Hopkins demonstrated in business after business that a true concern for the needs of the customer always yields success. Always.

Positioning is what happens when a company sets out to meet a consumer need, succeeds in doing so and communicates it well through advertising and public relations. Still, Ries and Trout deserve reading and contain some valuable insights. One of my favorite chapters is titled, "Those little ladders in your head."

In it, Ries and Trout discuss the natural mental process of merit ordering. In every business category, we rank the goods and services on ladders. On the soft drink ladder for example, most of us would place Coca-Cola on the top rung with Pepsi-Cola on the second rung. The next few rungs would probably differ by region but would no doubt be occupied by Dr. Pepper, 7-Up, Canada Dry and some brand of root beer.

"A competitor that wants to increase its share of the business must either dislodge the brand above it (a task that is usually impossible)," they tell us, "or somehow relate its brand to the other company's position."

As examples, they cite off-track betting, lead-free gasoline and sugar-free soda. That kind of list could go on and on, with decaffeinated coffee, no-alcohol beer, plus legions of non-fat and low-fat this and that. These are, in fact, not positions but product attributes.

True positioning requires abandoning the old ladders in people's heads and building a brand new one with your product at the top. Ries and Trout might respond that a person's mind has room for only so many ladders and they would be right. However, if your ladder is of more interest to him, he will toss an old one away in favor of it. Did Starbucks merely open a chain of coffee houses or did they create a new ladder? Did Macintosh just build another computer or did they build a new ladder? How about Chrysler's PT Cruiser?

People don't talk about meeting at the coffeehouse, they talk about meeting at Starbucks. They don't work on a computer, they work on a Mac. And the PT Cruiser? It's not a car, it's a PT.

Building a new ladder requires creativity. It can be primarily in initial design, like Macintosh or PT Cruiser, or in execution, like Starbucks. Or it can be in the way an existing product is presented to the world, such as 7-Up the Uncola.

If you want to move up your category ladder but find your way blocked by a major competitor who is impossible to dislodge, build a new ladder.

How? By discovering what the consumer wants from you and deliver it in a manner that surprises and delights her.

There are lots of examples of doing it backwards, ie. companies offering consumers what they wanted them to buy but consumers had no interest in:

Remember Xerox Computers? Kodak Instant Cameras?

About the same time, advertising agencies began to pitch what they called, "The Big Idea." Many of the ideas they presented as examples of this, however, were decidedly small. I remember, for example, sitting in a room filled with Ogilvy and Mather executives as one of our number proudly showed us the campaign for Pepperidge Farm Bread. The commercial he seemed most proud of was one in which an invented character named Titus Moody went around in a horse-drawn delivery van extolling the virtue of the product to a young boy who somehow managed not to tell Mr. Moody to leave him the hell alone. All of this was capped with the stunning assertion that "Pepperidge Farm Remembers."

This was described as a Big Idea. Of course it was anything but. However, it was the equal of many campaigns from many agencies that purported to make the same claim.

In fairness to Ogilvy and Mather, let me tell you about a truly Big Idea they had for Shell Oil in the Seventies. It was a time of gasoline shortages in which the major oil companies could not advertise gasoline. An art director named John Geyer and I had the idea (not a particularly big one) that we could get Shell to spend money on newspaper advertising if we presented it as a public service. We gave them ads on "How To Buy Tires," and "How To Choose a Motor Oil." Shell liked the idea because it also allowed them to run an ad on "How To Choose The Right Gasoline For Your Car" in which they introduced a new brand called, oxymoron aside, Super Regular.

The campaign met with some success and Shell enjoyed a small upward bump in the way they were perceived by consumers.

Later, at a meeting in Ogilvy's Houston office, a media wizard they had flown in from New York, and whose name I have long since forgotten, suggested a revolutionary idea: instead of newspaper ads, we would produce "how-to" booklets that the consumer could only obtain by coming to a Shell station. Then we would advertise the free booklets on television! Please understand that, at the time, all oil companies felt constrained from using television to drive business to their stations because they were not to advertise gasoline. Shell would drive people to their stations not to buy gasoline but to pick up free copies of booklets. If they bought gasoline while they were there, hey, We couldn't stop them.

That was a Big Idea.

I can't claim it. In fact, I left Ogilvy before the campaign was even written, much less approved. The work was done by Geyer, Bruce Silverman, Joe Kilgore and Paul Norris. But I did get to admire it. The commercials were not inspired or even particularly good, from a creative point-of-view, but they were a stunning success.

TIP 4: Instead of asking how we can sell this product to the consumer, ask first what we can offer the consumer that will truly be of value to him. Then you'll find your Big Idea.

VII

Short Term Profit Over Image

During the Seventies, there was a great deal of what was then called "Image Advertising." The theory was that, if people liked the image your company projected, they would be more likely to buy your product. More often they were intended to kite the company's stock and pump up the executives' egos. This led to a plethora of expensive commercials and campaigns that said little and left the viewers without a clue as to what was expected of them. In fact, the commercials probably did more for the advertising agencies, who showed them off to other prospective clients, than they ever did for the advertiser. Perhaps because of this, perhaps because wiser heads prevailed, or perhaps because stockholders revolted—most likely a combination of all of the above—image advertising soon fell into disrepute, but the pendulum swung back too far in the other direction.

The Eighties brought a demand for immediate profits. This shifted companies away from traditional advertising and into promotions. Strategies that were once used to introduce a product, or push up a sagging sales curve, now came to be used as its sole driving force. The strategy for a coupon ad shifted from trial to redemption. In short, we aren't just trying to attract new users to our product, we are trying to get existing users to redeem the coupon and use it, as well. There were giveaways, sweepstakes and games, all designed to sell as much product as possible in the current quarter.

As a result, brand loyalty, already declining due to the constant demand for attention from new products and new entries in various categories, went into free-fall.

America's automobile industry was particularly guilty. The move away from quality, and the image it projected, to rebates and price drops, opened the gates of the country to a flood of imports that left Detroit reeling.

Please don't misunderstand my point here. I am not saying that it was a swing to rebates and other promotions that led to the decline of America's auto industry in the Eighties. It was, in fact, placing short term profit over the customers' desire for quality, manifesting itself in, as a single example, the shifting of ad dollars into promotions, that was the villain.

The net result was that brand loyalty went into the toilet.

Let me fall back briefly on my own experience. The marketing director decided that Pearle Optical needed a "branding" campaign (since "image" had fallen into disrepute, a new word had to be coined to convey the same need for an attractive personality in which to present the company, the preferred word was "branding." I had a friend who made quite a name for himself by pushing a method he called "power branding." It all meant the same thing).

Pearle also had its franchisees to satisfy and they wanted immediate sales, long term needs be damned.

We discovered that Pearle was the largest purveyor of eyewear in the country. So we came up with the line, "The Eyes of America." More people trusted Pearle than any other company in the category, we said, and for good reason. The reasons were pretty much the same as any competitor could claim—designer eyewear, wide selection, etc.—but we were saying it better. We were taking the leadership position in a category in which no one had ever claimed it.

All well and good, except that the marketing director also insisted we use the same commercials to carry promotional messages. Then the plan to run the branding campaign exclusively for several months before returning to promotional advertising was junked. As a result, the leadership message was never heard over the BOGO (buy one, get one free) offer. A unique branding opportunity was lost. The marketing director, one in a series, by the way, soon departed. And Lenscrafters took over the number one position.

Many of the promotional techniques had originally been developed by Claude Hopkins as a way to introduce and augment a branding effort. But the promotions of the Eighties and early Nineties were entirely price-driven. Hopkins himself maintained that price was rarely a determining factor in a buying decision. Yet price-off had become the war cry of American advertisers.

When advertisers came to realize that, thanks to their own efforts, consumers were ignoring any form of brand loyalty in favor of who had the lowest price at the moment, they began to see the damage they had done to themselves. At the same time, they noticed that a few well-positioned and well-branded products were making an enormous impact on the market.

VIII

Hal Riney Takes Us Back To Branding

The most important single figure in the move back toward branding is a San Francisco adman named Hal Riney.

Until Riney's ascent, most branding was image-driven dreck transparent to any six year old. It took the form of chest-thumping, usually anthem music accompanied by a voice-over (think the late Orson Welles) telling us how hard the advertiser is working to build a better world.

The first commercial I ever saw from Hal Riney was for Crocker Bank. It was so simple, a young couple gets married and heads off for their honeymoon while the Carpenters sing, "We've Only Just Begun." The copy tells us that they'll need a good bank like Crocker. After seeing it for the first time, I realized why I hated jingles. Jingles are songs about product benefits and songs about product benefits are inherently silly and stupid. "We've Only Just Begun" wasn't about Crocker Bank. Never mentioned it. It was about young people starting out together in life.

Like many other Riney commercials, this one has often been called gooey or sentimental. I disagree. Beneath the romantic song and the beautiful wedding is the disquieting feeling we all have when witnessing such a scene; life is tough and these kids haven't the slightest idea of what they are in for. It's this concern that sets us up for the kill. Crocker Bank can help them find their way.

Hal Riney admits that his work is often emotional and defends it as such. The content, he tells us, must often be rational. The delivery, on the other hand, should contain emotion. Not every time, he adds, but more often than not.

He is also the author of some very funny commercials, such as the campaign for Bartles and Jaymes wine coolers. These were not emotional in the sense of the Crocker Bank commercial. But the two had something in common. We recognized ourselves or people we knew or situations we had experienced in them. Bartles and Jaymes weren't just a couple of old hicks sitting on a front porch. They were everyman working hard to produce the best possible product, being befuddled by the demands of contemporary marketing, and wishing to thank the people who enjoyed their work. "Thank you for your support."

What makes Riney's work so successful in so many cases is his ability to express values on behalf of his clients that are shared by an overwhelming number of the people he is trying to reach. There are hundreds of sentimental, gooey commercials that never make an impact. They fail because they are both shallow and predictable. Cute kids and puppies. Riney prefers old dogs and geezers. It is reaching beneath the surface things we hold in common (we all like puppies and kids) to the more deeply held feelings and beliefs that makes Riney's work so unforgettable and motivating.

We often hear that he uses a lot of "western" imagery, but the shared values he uses to connect us to what he is selling are not necessarily particular to the western part of the United States. It is true that we have graced this one area with some of our most cherished values through western movies. But hard work accompanied by pride in what we produce, integrity, love of family, loyalty and compassion play equally well in the East. These are values we all share, values we all admire and aspire to, even if we don't always live up to them.

Many of our shared values are ineffable, which is also why so much of Riney's most memorable work is in television, where he can use scenery and music to communicate as well. He does not hit us with a sledge hammer. He is subtle and quiet, as one should be when reaching out to touch us at such deep levels.

Today, the use of shared values, as Riney has demonstrated, provides the most effective approach to branding available. What Riney has done is to humanize his client and place their products squarely on the consumer's side of the net, not by appealing solely to his or her wants or needs but to the values they hold in common.

An early example of this is cited in David Ogilvy's book, *Ogilvy On Advertising.* It's a commercial for Blitz-Weinhard Beer written by Riney when he ran Ogilvy's San Francisco office. Blitz was a regional beer in Oregon. The voice is that of an Oregon rancher as we watch him at work. He tells us that he, like his father before him, values the "natural way." Blitz is brewed the natural way. Then he closes by making the connection between the beer and the values particular to that part of the nation: "Blitz country, natural country, natural beer." You won't find any phonies drinking Blitz-Weinhard.

Perhaps Riney's most well-known work, however, was for Gallo Wines. The Gallo Brothers, Ernest and Julio, were generally considered to be difficult clients. They took a great deal of pride in their product.

Despite this, Gallo Wines were not highly regarded. Riney designed a campaign that would change this forever.

To begin with, there was a great deal of argument about just what constituted a great wine and just how it could be produced. The soil in California. The grapes. The casks in which it fermented. The timing with which it was handled. Plus any number of other processes. Rather than identify a single benefit, or Unique Selling Proposition, Riney embraced them all as examples of values we share: the integrity of work, the refusal to compromise quality, pride in the results of our efforts, and an unfailing dedication to our customers. He began with a swell of music accompanied by beautiful cinematography on the wine-making process, then closed with this simple toast from the people of Gallo to their customers: "All The Best."

Next, Riney took on politics and produced a commercial for the re-election of President Ronald Reagan that has become a classic. It began with an early morning wide shot of Everytown as the voice-over intones, "it's morning in America." With an economy of words, it reminded us of the "malaise" the country had been in before Reagan's election and how much better we felt about ourselves now that Reagan was in the White House. There have been four presidential elections since and not one of them has produced a single commercial of this stature. Riney's political advertising rose above the negative attack form so common at the time, and more common since then, to touch on a subject everyone cares deeply about: our shared values.

Joel Raphaelson, a former creative director at O&M and the son of one of filmdom's greatest writers, Samson Raphaelson, once expressed an opinion that was quoted in Ogilvy On Advertising.

"In the past just about every advertiser has assumed that in order to sell his goods he has to convince consumers that his product is *superior* to his competitor's.

"This may not be necessary. It may be sufficient to convince consumers that your product is *positively good.* If the consumer feels certain that your product is good and feels uncertain about your competitor's, he will buy yours.

"If you and your competitors all make excellent products, don't try to imply that your product is *better,* Just say what is good about your product—*and do a clearer, more honest, more informative job of saying it.*

"If this theory is right, sales will swing to the marketer who does the best job of creating confidence that his product is *positively good."*

What better way is there to say your product is positively good than through shared values? By the way, all of the Italics in the quote are Joel's. I worked for Joel for several years and we never agreed on the use of Italics and underlines. Reflecting back, I think he was right.

Roy Spence, president of GSD&M, states unequivocally that, "what your company stands for is more important than what it makes." Again, shared values.

Needless to say, shared values advertising is unlikely to work, and in most cases will backfire, when you have no values to share. If a consumer reads your shared value ad and then discovers that you've plundered your employees' profit sharing plan, polluted the environment, or had layoffs to enhance the bottom line while your top executives held to exorbitant salaries and benefits, you may have done more harm than good.

When advertisers witnessed both the destruction an over-emphasis on promotions could wreak, plus the brand-building potential of an approach like Riney's, they decided that they, too, needed a branding campaign. Unfortunately, most advertising agencies were no longer prepared to offer them.

IX

The Death Of Campaigns

Several years ago, a creative director at a major national agency told me, "we don't believe in campaigns anymore. Each ad must stand on its own."

Of course each ad must stand on its own, I answered, but to forego the synergy of a well-executed campaign is wasteful.

His answer was that the format demanded by a campaign stifled the creativity of his people. If they came up with five or six really creative ads, each bearing no resemblance to the other, why not run them all? Why kill good ads just because they don't conform to a campaign? What he was arguing against was discipline. What he wanted was "creative freedom." To what end? you may well ask. The answer is simple: to win awards.

Let me say a few words in favor of campaigns before we go on, though it probably brands me as an old fogey. First, there is the afore-mentioned synergy. Ads and commercials that look alike and attack the same proposition from different angles form a whole that is greater than the sum of the parts. In addition, consumers begin to look forward to the next commercial as they would the next installment of a story. A common look and feel in the advertising builds a repository of good will that, as branding, carries the product over the rough spots when competitors use price-driven promotions and give-aways to build share.

TIP #5: A campaign, as opposed to a series of unrelated ads or commercials, is the best and least expensive way to build and maintain brand loyalty. Using shared values is the best way to build a campaign.

X

The Dysfunctional Culture Of
Today's Advertising Agency

Would a writer or art director really subvert a client's best interests in order to win an award? You bet he would. But before you condemn these people, try to understand the culture that drives them. First, they often have a willing accomplice in the agency's management. In fact, the lengths to which agencies will go to produce advertising that is of more benefit to the agency or the individual creative person than to the client is one of the business' dirty little secrets. This insistence by management that the creative people, on one hand, win awards at all costs and, on the other, produce work that will satisfy the client, often leaves the creative department a hotbed of cynicism. But let's back up and start from the beginning.

Advertising agencies usually win business through presentations. These are known as dog-and-pony shows in the industry. The winner is not always the best agency, but the best presenter. This would make a lot of sense if you could get the agency's presentation team to visit every customer and potential customer in America with their show. Failing that, it is a really stupid way to choose a business partner who will represent you to your most important audience. Powerful presenters have more in common with stand-up comics. motivational speakers and televangelists than with advertising giants like Riney, Bernbach and Ogilvy.

Next, the presentation will always comprise a reel of commercials the agency has done for existing clients, though not always. I once watched an agency present commercials and case histories for five clients, never mentioning that they had lost three of them. The commercials they show potential clients will be chosen for their humor or immediate impact, not the marketing savvy and creative thinking that went into them. For all anyone watching may know, every one of the commercials on the reel may have been completely ineffective.

Harry McMahan, a columnist for Ad Age Magazine once took the Clio Festival, advertising's imitation of the Academy Awards, to task for just this reason. Agencies that won four of the Clio Awards had lost the accounts, he wrote. Another winner had gone out of business. Still another had refused to put his winning entry on the air. In fact, McMahan wrote, of the 81 commercials picked as classics of the past, 36 of the agencies involved had lost the account of gone out of business.

I am not against the Clio festival and I am strongly in favor of inno-vation and creativity in advertising. But I am even more strongly in favor of advertising effectiveness and no one can assess a commercial's effectiveness merely from watching it during a presentation.

The content of a presentation is even more dubious. When an agency discovers that a particular account may be up for grabs, they spend a great deal of time trying to find out what that account, that potential client, might want. I have heard many agency leaders boldly proclaim that they have passed on a particular account because "we didn't feel it was a good fit." I have never seen it done, however, and usually it was an excuse for having failed to make a good impression.

Agencies will, generally, do or say anything that is not illegal in order to win an account. I started to add "immoral" but I thought better of it. Tracy-Locke, which was later absorbed into DDB Needham, once ran an ad that proclaimed, "we will kill for your business." Knowing the management at the time, I don't doubt they would have.

If a potential client is reputed to have a love for research, most agencies will wax poetic on their research capability and how they are, in their hearts, research-driven. Often clients leave their previous agency due to poor service on the account. If a pitching agency finds this out, they will emphasize the great lengths they will go to in order to better serve their clients. Often they promise, "we will go into your stores (or, worse, your factory) and work alongside your people in order to better understand your business." Be assured that the person making the promise is never the one who fulfills it.

As an aside, I once proposed to an agency management committee that we simply tell every potential client the same thing: who we are and what we can do for them. Better they know right away, I said, than find out later and decide they don't like us. It made a great deal of sense to me, since our history with clients was one of long marriages or quick divorces, but my fellow committee members looked at me as if I'd grown a second head.

Something you will not hear an agency promise, however, is that they will come up with some really wacky commercials that their 24-year-old art director can brag about to his friends at the local coffee house. Yet that is going to be a major part of the ensuing effort. Why? Because the president or CEO or creative director of the agency has told the 24-year-old art director that they support his desire to do wacky commercials, regardless of the client. They do this in order to placate the 24-year-old art director and keep him or her from leaving and taking a job at another agency that makes the same promise in a more convincing manner.

Should the agency get the new account, based on, say, a promise of greater service, there will be much celebrating in the halls. Various employees will look at this new account as fresh meat and be anxious to claim their share. Then the promises of the presentation will be lost as the lead presenter goes on to the next pitch and the people to whom the account is assigned begin to sharpen their individual axes.

The creative people, the writer and the art director, plus all their supervisory levels, are looking for opportunities to impress their peers. You will never hear a creative person say, "I'm so proud; my commercial resulted in a three percent share increase in the first quarter."

You may well hear them say, "my commercial took gold at the local Addys (awards) and has a good shot at going to Cannes."

This is not just egotism. It is, for the individual writer or art director, good business. A gold medal in a national show can mean a big salary bump or a new job somewhere else for considerably more money. If that sounds disloyal, first consider that loyalty is a two-way street. Layoffs are common at advertising agencies of all sizes. In many cases, the longer you stay at a particular agency, the greater your chances of getting laid off. And, in this business, they don't care if you're 60 years old, are suffering from multiple sclerosis or have three kids in college. The agency business is, for the most part, heartless. I added "for the most part" because, an eternal optimist, I want to leave room for the exception. After all, I was lucky enough to work for Sam Bloom.

Occasionally, this sort of heartlessness can come back to haunt an agency. For example, I knew an account person who was laid off without warning, along with several others, simply to improve the agency's bottom line that quarter. The agency, however, had failed to notify the account executive's client, who happened to think very highly of her and resented her loss. He wasn't notified because he was a lowly brand manager. Two years later, he was promoted to marketing vice president, a position from which he slowly and painfully tortured and fired the agency. More often, however, there are no repercussions.

So the writer or art director looks at the agency and its clients and asks, would they extend themselves for me? The answer is usually "no" (there are some wonderful exceptions). So, he or she asks, why should I extend myself for them. Better I should build a book filled with the kind of ads that win bigger jobs, commercials that wow, plus a buttload of awards that whoever interviews me at the next agency will drool over.

That sounds like a plan for a young person but makes no sense for older writers and art directors, you say. Well, I answer, what older writers and art directors? There are not many and it's not because younger people are more in tune with the market. That's baloney. When you see an industry ridding itself of its most experienced and settled people, you can bet the bean counters are behind it.

If you're old, you're out.

Okay, this is going to sound like sour grapes, since I am officially considered "old" in the agency business (in my heart I am about 28). But I can't do anything about that and it's important for you to know about this development. Think it over. If it still sounds like sour grapes to you, so be it. But I have to tell you, I really enjoy working for myself. I choose it seven years ago because I noticed that clients generally want and respect experience in their advertising counselors. I have no regrets. That said, we plow on.

About the same time advertisers learned to maximize short-term profits by diverting branding dollars to promotions, they noticed that advertising agencies were drooling over them like a pack of hungry dogs. Agencies were so devoted to capitalized billing that they would accept virtually any compensation agreement, no matter how degrading. The standard agency commission of 15 percent was cut, sometimes by two-thirds. Many agencies and their clients settled on monthly fees which were intended to cover the hours worked by agency personnel on the account and eliminated commissions altogether.

Instead of banding together to resist this downturn in their income, agencies vied with each other, to the delight of their clients, to see how willing a partner they could become in their own undoing. Of course, the money had to come from somewhere and the answer was obvious. Ever since the Sixties, advertising had maintained a fascination with "youth culture." What advertisers would object if they found themselves across the table from someone who not only knew the market, but was part of it?

Younger people without mortgages, kids in college or daughters who were about to be married could be paid less. David Ogilvy once complained that the lowered compensation made agencies unable to hire the best business school graduates as they had in the past. These young men and women, he said, were now more likely to go to work on the client side. Suddenly, the agency was being outsmarted by its own client.

There was a time when an MBA degree was required to get an interview for an account executive position in a major agency. Now those jobs are likely to be held by former clerks and secretaries.

Some of the first casualties were in broadcast production. I knew several experienced producers who were fired and replaced by inexperienced younger people at half the salary. One, a producer hired by a Dallas agency and moved from New York, was let go some years later and replaced by a receptionist. That agency's broadcast production staff was so young and inexperienced that they were referred to as "the produc-erettes" by the local broadcast community.

In the Creative Department, the change was catastrophic. Instead of seasoned pros you had youngsters who would normally be serving an apprenticeship, now standing at the helm. They were not interested in what Hopkins or Ogilvy or even Bernbach or Riney had to say. They wanted to do it their way.

In account service, where once you had men and women with MBA's and years of experience to contain some of the creative people's more irrational impulses, you now had former secretaries who were intimi-dated by creatives. What's more, all of these people, sensing theirs was not a permanent position, as witnessed by the frequency of layoffs, saw no point in struggling toward a solution for all of this chaos; it wasn't worth the effort.

In many cases, agency management did not understand the depth of the problem between creative people, the account service people and the client. Unlike the pioneers of modern advertising, most of the men and women running today's agencies couldn't actually create an ad themselves and most know nothing about television and film produc-tion.

I have seen several cases in which the client simply took the creative decision-making away from the agency. This may seem logical to the clients, but the idea of having non-creative people in charge of the cre-ative process simply doesn't work.

Clients are more and more likely to reassign media planning and buying either to their own internal people or to an independent media placement company. The reasons mirror the problems we've discussed in the creative department. Also, the profit crunch has resulted in an overworked media department that no longer has time for in-depth, ongoing analysis. My own media planner and buyer insists on getting a full 15 percent commission. In exchange, he monitors radio and television networks and stations on a daily, if not hourly, basis. All of our clients have a "Fire Sale Fund" and give him the authority to make opportunistic buys, as long as they fit into set, already agreed-upon parameters. Contrasting this with the traditional plan it, buy it, then forget it method, we can add from 30 to 50 percent in value to clients' media budgets. No agency can afford to make this effort for their clients if their commissions are discounted.

As a result, everything the advertisers have saved on commissions has been lost in spades to less effective creative and media.

TIP #6: Compensate your agency well, then expect full service from seasoned professionals, and accept nothing less.

Let me also defend my creative brethren. Today, these often undertrained and ill-prepared young people are expected to provide the client with sensible advertising that he or she will like and approve, and, at the same time, win awards given by people who don't even bother to ask about the effectiveness of an ad or commercial, preferring to judge it solely on how it makes them feel.

The long term effect is that agency people are angry and management prefers to bury its head in the sand. I know of one agency that sent out a questionnaire to gauge morale, promising that every answer would be kept confidential. One creative person, foolish enough to believe that, ending up squirming in his seat while the president of the agency read his remarks to a gathering of officers and then remarked, "well, there's one guy who just doesn't get it."

Indeed, somebody certainly doesn't get it.

When the tail wags the dog.

Decades ago, art directors clubs began to sponsor award shows in an effort to improve the quality of advertising graphics. At the time it started, it was desperately needed. In time, they added awards for copy in order to win the copywriter to their side. That may sound strange to art directors nowadays, but in that long-ago time, copywriters straddled the fence between account service and creative. In fact, there was a position known as "copy/contact" filled by a writer who also managed, or helped manage, the account.

Once the alliance was formed, some art directors' clubs became creative clubs, witness the One Club in New York and the Dallas-Fort Worth Society of Visual Communications.

The American Advertising Federation also had its own awards show, The Addys. While not regarded with the reverence of the One Show, the art directors shows or the CA (Communication Arts Magazine awards), creative people had become so hungry for esteem that they flooded it with entries as well. The Clios, mentioned earlier, have a strange history. At one time, it was considered the single most important awards show. Then there was a scandal about mishandled funds and the show disappeared. It has re-appeared but is far less prestigious.

Years ago, I shocked a group of friends by admitting that the main reason I went to awards shows was to find and hire new creative people. Now it's a common practice. The more well known creative people are, the more money they are going to make. And the best way to become well-known is to win awards. The more the better. The more prestigious the better. And few will let small considerations like the well-being of the client stand in their way.

Why should they? Clients rarely form bonds with their creative team and agencies feel free to lay them off at a whim. Circumstances drive creative people to protect and promote themselves and awards are one very good way to do it. Self-preservation demands that they put their own, and their families' interests ahead of their clients. Their careers depend entirely upon their books and awards. Until this changes, the culture will remain dysfunctional.

The question always arises: don't award-winning ads also win at the cash register, and the answer is that they do. Sometimes. And sometimes they don't. The point here is that the objective should be to turn on the consumer first. Whether or not it turns on the judges of the awards shows should be one of the least important objectives.

Bernbach saw this day coming years ago when he said, "Today, everybody is talking about 'Creativity' and frankly, that's got me worried. I fear we keep the good taste and lose the sell. I fear all the sins we may commit in the name of 'Creativity.' I fear we may be entering an age of phonies."

Welcome to the Age of Phonies.

Today a major agency will spend well over $100,000 a year on award shows and will probably have a person whose sole responsibility is to make sure the right entries get there at the right time. An ad agency has only one source of income, its clients. So guess who pays the $100,000. The same people who get ignored when the choice is between an award-winning approach and one that will create demand.

This is not to blame awards shows for the ills of the agency business. The purpose of these shows, at least most of them, is to award exceptional graphics, photography, illustration, cinematography, design and typography. And that is all they are intended to do. They never claim to sort out and award the most effective advertising. In short, they do what they are intended to do very well. They do not do what has, unfortunately, come to be expected of them.

TIP #7: Demand involvement in the awards show process. They are, after all, your ads and commercials.

Speaking of phonies, another book could be written on the strange world of television commercial production. The cost of the average national television commercial is over $250,000. In 1983, Ogilvy called the average cost of television commercials "the great scandal." Back then, it was only $60,000.

Directors of television commercials love to strut about as if they were film directors. Some, like Ridley Scott, make the jump. But most are not remotely talented enough. Still they demand enormous day rates and live in huge homes in Beverly Hills. They have representatives, usually lovely and expensively dressed young women who criss-cross the country, staying in luxury hotels, buying lavish meals and running up insane bar bills with the creative people they are trying to impress.

The more expensive the director, the less time he will have for your project. These men and women are masters of patronizing their clients.

Ask them to consider your point of view and you'll be met with a sympathetic smile, as if you were a drooling idiot, even if the concept behind the commercial is entirely yours. As far as I know, none of these self-absorbed ego-freaks have ever come up with a single advertising idea, but once your idea lands in their laps, it's all theirs. Try to interfere with their "vision" and you're likely be taken aside and instructed in the proper manner in which one conducts oneself on a shoot, either by their producer or—and this is really maddening—your own.

Unlike film directors, many commercial directors neither demand nor even want the first cut. They don't want the second cut either. In fact, once you've moved into the post-production phase, it's highly unlikely that you'll ever see him or her again. Oh, and that production company producer who welcomed you so warmly a few days before and handed you a coffee mug with your name on it? You've seen the last of that person, too.

Creative people and agency producers play willingly into the "great scandal." In fact, they are often co-conspirators. They insist on staying at the finest hotels and, when the production company buys one expensive meal after another, they never stop and ask where the money is coming from. They just keep eating.

There's a strong possibility you'll encounter overages as well. Throughout the shoot, you'll notice the agency producer and the production company producer huddled off to the side. They are discussing the overages. They are talking about all of the things that one of them, or both, forgot to mention and how the cost of those things is spiraling out of control. When you see them doing this, walk past, smile and say, "we're not paying any overages." You'll love the reaction.

The net result is that you'll end up with a commercial which may or may not resemble what you set out to do and will cost far more than the original estimate, which was excessive to begin with. Complain and you'll once more be met with patronizing smiles while someone takes you aside to remind you of how important the director is. The client be damned.

This, of course, is the reason that the number of commercial directors has multiplied like rabbits in a deserted garden. It's easy work. You don't seem to need much talent. And the money flows like water during the monsoon.

Am I being unfair to the really terrific directors out there? Of course I am. But. as a whole, the commercial production industry deserves a verbal trashing, and everyone involved in it knows that's true.

Maybe your agency acknowledges that there are some problems but says there is little that can be done. Well, I know what can be done and in a later chapter I'll share it with you.

TIP #8: Demand that your agency producer provide a list of "A" and "B" directors, explain if and when a more expensive director is bid, and make sure that all contingencies are covered in advance; you will not countenance overages.

XI

Irony and the Drug Culture

In the late Sixties, drugs became a part of our national culture. To be considered hip, television variety shows, popular at the time, had to make veiled, and sometimes not so veiled, references to drugs, followed by knowing looks and laughs. Drug terms such as "rush," "high," and "freak out" became part of our everyday idiom. Smoking dope was merely an entry into hip society. Then more intense hallucinogens like LSD and mescaline. Then crystal meth. Cocaine followed early in the next decade. And we were on a drug binge like we've never seen before in this country. Alcohol remained the friendly fellow traveler in this new culture. For those quite reasonably afraid of the newly available psychotropics, the comfortable alternative of getting drunk remained, if not terribly hip, then at least acceptable.

Advertising people, particularly creative people, were desperate to be hip. This desperation was reflected in some of the worst advertising of the time, as supposedly psychedelic colors washed across our television screen and images of cartoonish flowers and polka-dot mushrooms lurked on the borders of retail ads, all to say, "hey, we're hip, too" and, by implication, either we do drugs, too, or we approve of drug-taking. If you find it hard to believe that popular media promoted drug use, review old tapes of "Laugh-In" and "The Smothers Brothers Comedy Hour."

The split between account management people and the newly-aligned forces of writer-and-art director became even more profound. The creative people dismissed account people as "empty suits." In return, account people referred to the creative department as "the zoo."

As you might expect, the one who suffered most from this conflict was the client.

The euphoria produced by regular drug-consumption, followed by the inevitable comedown, gave birth to an attitude of derision toward society in general. Some of this irony was well-deserved and the conformity of the preceding decade was an easy target. But the net effect was to associate hipness with irony. The more positive side of the awakening of the Sixties, as epitomized by John Denver's music, for example, was written off as saccharine or cheesy. The tone shifted from Denver to Alice Cooper to Kiss and, it seems, inevitably to Marilyn Manson.

History, at the same time, played its own part. The idealistic Sixties became the disillusioned Seventies as the Pentagon Papers revealed the cynicism behind the management of the Viet Nam War, followed by the seemingly unending series of scandals lumped under the label "Watergate." A weary sense of irony became a safe haven in turbulent times.

To the youthful creative person yearning to be perceived as hip, especially by the Hollywood community, the urge toward irony is difficult to resist. And the agency business, ever desirous of appearing at one with youth culture, follows. We now have the bizarre picture of agency creative people driving their BMW convertibles down the Hollywood Freeway listening devotedly to the rhymed threats and complaints of psychotic ghetto gangsters and describing it as "music." The advertising they produce is equally bizarre.

Take, for example the television commercial for a credit card in which a father attempts to discuss money with his adolescent son. The father's attempts morph into "blah, blah, blah, blah," while the kid continues to stare at a television screen. completely ignoring him. After the father leaves, the son dismisses him with a disdainful remark. And, guess what? the target of this spot is the father! How bizarre is it to run a television spot in which you insult your target audience!

At one time a client might have depended on his account person to prevent such mistakes, but consider how our account service staff has changed as a result of lowered commissions and, therefore, lower salaries. We now have younger account people who are oftentimes as anxious to appear ironic and hip as their creative peers.

Symbolism over strategy.

Mary Wells Lawrence was an icon of the Creative Revolution in advertising. She no longer feels she could succeed in the business. In a rare interview, Lawrence said her work was always based on strategy. Today's advertising is based on symbolism, she said. And, she added, she didn't think she could do that.

She couldn't do it, she feels, because it's not effective advertising.

Phyllis Robinson, once Bernbach's copy chief and a member of the Copywriters Hall of Fame, takes an even dimmer view of the new symbol-over-strategy creative work. She believes it's overrun by technique and "smart-ass, wise guy stuff."

"Everything now is so frenzied and so obscure," she once told Ad week Magazine. "It's sad because it's a reflection of our culture."

XII

The Peter Principle in the Mega-Agency

On the off-chance that you've never heard of the Peter Principle, it is simply that, in bureaucratic organizations, people tend to rise to their level of incompetence. Since demotions are unheard-of in this type of organization, the individual remains at his level of incompetence.

The Peter Principle was first introduced by Lawrence J. Peter in his book of the same title. The principle is based on the observation that in a bureaucracy new employees typically start in the lower ranks, but when they prove to be competent in the task to which they are assigned, they get promoted to a higher rank. This process continues until the employee reaches a position just above his or her level of competency. The result is that the higher levels are filled by incompetent people.

There is another not-so-well stated principle of which we are all aware that pertains equally well to bureaucratic organizations: *The bigger the organizations the more the sycophants will succeed.*

However, this does not preclude their success in entrepreneurial organizations. Most entrepreneurs—and all of the major agencies were at one time run by entrepreneurs—turn one of two ways as their company develops:

1. They hire people they consider even more able than themselves and willingly share power with them.
2. They surround themselves with yes-men and sycophants.

If they do the former, they tend to become like Sam Bloom, wise mentors who are greatly respected by both clients and associates. If they choose the latter path, they end up working themselves into a death trance because they have surrounded themselves with people whose only real talent is for kissing the rear end of whoever is in charge.

I mention both the Peter Principle and the Sycophant Principle because all of the major advertising agencies have become bureaucracies. And all are subject to both.

The Peter Principle is inherent in the agency business. If a writer proves to be brilliant at his task, he will be promoted to associate creative director and will be diverted from his writing chores to engage in supervision and administration. If he continues to do well, he will go on to become a creative director, where his creative involvement will be limited to approving, or disapproving, other people's work because administration and supervision have begun to overwhelm him. Since the creative department must have a place at the management table, he may have to become the member of one or two committees that will suck even more of his time away. Now, of course, the brilliant copywriter no longer writes copy. His time is taken entirely by chores for which he has no proven competence while his salary has skyrocketed. Creative people have begun to complain that they never see him. Account managers complain that he spends too little time with their clients. And management is convinced that he values creative originality too highly over other considerations. Most of us reach our level of incompetence right about here, Some go on to become executive creative directors and do even worse. The same is true of the gifted account manager. She is a strategic genius and is superb at handling even the most difficult and demanding client. So let's promote her to a position in which she spends less time strategizing and rarely, if ever, meets with a client.

Since the problem is truly inherent in the business, agencies found their individual ways of coping with it. Bill Hill, the creative director at the Bloom Agency, had a right-hand man named Arlen Bryant who kept him from dropping the administrative and supervisory ball. David Ogilvy quickly turned his executive chores over to a brilliant array of men and women like Jock Elliott and Reva Korda.

Then problems began to worsen when many agency principles discovered they could make millions by taking their agencies public. Greed overtook the love of advertising, as well as good sense. Though it gave many the ability to live in relative splendor in Caribbean villas or along the coast of France, they lost control to the demands of shareholders. No longer could a contrarian like Claude Hopkins institute a radical new idea and see it work. Agencies now had to stick to "proven methods." Since no such thing exists, they found themselves imitating what worked for someone else. But it didn't matter, because the goal of the agency business had shifted from serving clients to serving our own bottom lines. Agencies merged and created mega-agencies. Mega-agencies in turn swallowed up independent agencies. With the dearth of creative ideas, caused by all this merging and swallowing, new independent agencies emerged and, in turn, were also swallowed. The bureaucracies grew and the problems caused by the Peter Principle and the Sycophant Principle steadily worsened. The history of advertising is filled with cranky geniuses whose intuitive skills would be completely lost in this new advertising structure. The Mega-Agency doesn't develop great talent; it drowns it.

In order to fool clients into believing there were no conflicting accounts within these mega-agencies—an absolute impossibility—mega-agency managements developed the fiction that all the agencies they controlled were, in fact, locally managed. Of course, they sent a team from the holding company to go over the books and advise the local management. And the sycophants, who always seem to have a clearer view of the future than the rest of us, cozied up to these important visitors. You can bet that, once the local management—the entrepreneurs who started the agency and then conspired in it's being gobbled up by the big guys—retired, the sycophants will be first in line for their jobs. More likely, many will have already left for higher positions in their "sister agencies."

TIP #9: Contest what your account managers have to say. If they won't stand up for their point-of-view, ask to have them replaced.

XIII

Salvaging The Wasted Half

If you read this and find fault with your advertising agency, the first impulse will be to replace it. That's not always a good idea. In most cases, you can create the kind of change in your existing agency that will maximum the effectiveness of your ad budget. Here's how:

Make sure your agency people know your company.

You assume they do, and they will assure you that they do. But their knowledge is often perfunctory at best. Chances are, these same people are working on several other pieces of business and don't have the time to get to know you in depth. Insist that this change, and do your part by making sure the agency is adequately compensated. As in so many things, in advertising you get what you pay for. Squeeze your agency on compensation and you'll be squeezed in return when it comes to advertising effectiveness.

Prepare an overview of your company and insist that everyone who works on your business be there for the presentation. Discuss problems and opportunities that may seem to lie outside the advertising venue. If they don't get involved and ask questions, if they don't suggest solutions to the problems, no matter how outlandish, dismiss them and ask the agency for a new team.

Get to know your agency people.

There is, in fact, no such thing as an advertising agency other than a collection of people who happen to be under one roof at a given time. An ad agency's only product is ideas and ideas come from people, not from institutions. Today, agencies hire and fire with such impunity that few clients have any real idea of who is creating their advertising. Sure, it may be presented by the same creative director as last time, but who is to say that it wasn't done by a team of juniors hidden in the bowels of the agency?

Make sure you are talking to the people who actually create your advertising. Get to know them personally. Call each of them when they're not expecting to hear from you. Kick around ideas with them. Once you find yourself with a creative and account service team that knows your business and works hard for it, protect them. Don't let them become the latest sacrifices to agency management's inability to meet projections demanded by their mega-agency overlords.

TIP # 10: Be sure your creative people know they're not just making ads; they're building your company.

Also, follow the tips in this book. Don't allow the creative people or the agency to put award shows and their personal books ahead of the needs of your company. Stop producers from using film production companies that overcharge and under-deliver. Turn down advertising that relies on irony and sarcasm or portrays your customer as a buffoon. Demand new ideas that have nothing to do with advertising. Discuss your company's mission statement and values and make sure your agency people take them seriously.

Making your agency perform at 100 percent may be difficult and cause some wrenching changes, but it will be worth it to you. Make sure it's worth it to your agency team, as well, by supporting them, which means protecting them from lay-offs and from overwork (be sure you know how many other accounts they're working on and just what they are), thank them for their efforts and work to make them understand that what they're doing is important, that they are not just laying bricks.

Process is important.

At one time, most agencies employed a process or system for creative development. Some still do. For most however, it has been reduced to account management filling out a form, which the client never sees, and delivering it to the creative department. Most of us in the creative side of the business would like to pretend that a more involved process isn't necessary because process involves a certain degree of discipline. We would like to be free of anything that we feel interferes with our spontaneity. Like most irrational beliefs, this is based on fear; fear that we won't be able to meet the criteria of the process, that somehow our cleverness will be overlooked or ignored because it didn't fit the process. But the process is important.

That having been said, it's possible to let the process overwhelm the work. One must ask the question:

Does this process aid our people and make their work better, or is it simply a management devise to control them and avoid any risk in the advertising they produce?

The Bloom Agency, now Publicis-Bloom, used to have a simple, three-step procedure for advertising development that remains the best I've seen. Each step required a sign-off by the client.

Step One, Industry Overview. A select committee would be assembled, people the account and creative team felt would be especially helpful for this particular client. There would be a short meeting to lay out the state of the industry in which our client worked and how he fit into it.

Step Two. Strategy Check. This meeting was run by the account management people. They laid out the strategy they had devised, and shared with their creative peers. The committee would listen and advise. This was not an approval process. It was a chance to get input from dispassionate experts. Opinions were shared. Ideas discussed. Then the team moved on to creative development.

Step Three. Creative Check. The creative team began by presenting a platform, a foundation for the work that was to follow, based on the strategy that had previously been discussed. Next, creative executions would be shown, in rough form, and discussed. This was not an invitation for others to participate in the creative process, and for good reason. First, creative done by committees is invariably bad creative. Second, non-creative people, when they have an idea, are so taken with themselves that a great deal of sensitivity, not to mention time, is lost of convincing them that their idea stinks. Also, it is not an approval process. Everyone at the meeting realizes that the team working directly on the account is best qualified to determine the best advertising for it. However, on several occasions, I saw work tossed out by the creative team due to some reservations expressed in the meeting.

Here's an important point: if creative was developed that was obviously brilliant but defied all the logic leading up to it, the account management team would gleefully rethink their strategy. Everything was subservient to the sudden flash of brilliance and inspiration.

It was difficult for creative people to throw away two or three week's work, and everyone had to be aware of this, especially the creative people themselves. That's why Bill Bernbach always carried a card that read, "Maybe They're Right." Even the best needed reminding.

For several years, Bloom, under the creative direction of Bill Hill and Don Bellisario and working within this system, turned out some of the most creative and effective advertising in the country. I recommend you show it to your agency. If they think they have one that's better, make them prove it.

Later, Sam Bloom began to withdraw and turn the business over to his son, Bob, who decided that the future of advertising was in packaged goods and drove his creative department toward the formulaic style employed by packaged goods advertisers at that time. He brought in copywriters and art directors experienced in that style, obviously not the most innovative people in the business, and the agency's creative reputation withered away. Bellisario went off to become a Hollywood legend and Hill left to form Levenson and Hill Advertising and Public Relations.

As we—the creative team of Bloom—broke apart, those of us who had participated in Bloom's glory days discovered something that creative people in other disciplines have also discovered to their dismay: we were far better together than we could ever be as individuals. Today's exceptional creative teams would do well to keep that in mind.

TIP #11: Whatever process your agency uses, make sure you, the client, are a part of it. Don't wait for the presentation of creative to find out where they are headed.

The agony and the new agency.

If all else fails, you may have to go through the agony of finding a new agency and hoping that you haven't made a mistake. There are lots of ways to do it, but the best possible one is the one you develop with your own company's needs in mind. That said, here are a few suggestions that will lessen the chances of disaster.

Do your own spade work. It's popular nowadays to use consultants in finding a new agency. Many of these people are quite good at what they do. My question, however, is whether a consultant can know more about you than you do? I can guarantee they rarely know squat about the agencies they interview. If not, this argues for either your doing this detailed chore yourself or at least maintaining a real depth of involvement throughout.

Don't be overly impressed by size. Large agencies will tell you that their media clout gives them a big advantage. Hal Riney points out that it is the client, not the agency, that carries the clout. Besides, outstanding creative will beat media clout any day.

Tell them you want to know who they are, not who they think you are. Years ago, agencies decided that they would succeed more in new business presentations if they kept the focus on the potential client rather than themselves. While this Dale Carnegie-style approach makes good sense in personal selling, it leaves a lot lacking in an advertising new business presentation. Tell them in advance that, while you'd love to see their thoughts and ideas regarding your company and its competitors, the primary purpose is for you to learn about them.

Ask tough questions. If they show you case histories, ask who specifically was responsible for these successes and whether they are still employed at the agency. Ask what their turnover rate is. Tell them to bring along the people who will actually be working on your business and ask to see the work these people have done in the past for other clients. Ask them questions about their work and their careers. And judge all the answers by the character they display as well the knowledge and creativity.

Turn your nose up at florid language. Ad agencies have been honing their presentation skills for decades and many have become masters of the form. If you're seeing more form than substance, ask for specifics. If they say, "we'll go the extra mile for you," ask exactly what that entails.

XIV

Radical Thinking: Do You Really Need An Advertising Agency?

In the past, there have only been two choices: an in-house agency and advertising department, or a traditional advertising agency. The latter has all the problems we've discussed so far. The former breaks apart on the shoals of tedium as your creative people grow weary of thinking about the same product day after day.

Now, however, there's a third way:

Create your own virtual agency.

Predictions of doom for the traditional advertising agency have been heard since the Seventies. So many, in fact, that some agencies have positioned themselves as somehow different, new and far better than those dinosaurs that preceded them. Look beneath the surface and you find the same old animal with a new coat of paint.

But the Internet is changing all that. Writers, art directors, account managers, media planners, research experts—all of these people can work together from across town or across the world. What's more, you only pay for their time and services when you're using them. So you don't end up paying for the leather couches in the agency foyer or the potted palms in the chairman's office. You pay only for what you need.

There have always been talented free-lance writers and art directors. Agencies would have you believe that these people are simply not good enough to join their ranks. If that were so, why do agencies turn to free-lancers so often themselves?

The truth is, most free-lancers are people who enjoy their craft and despair of agency politics. They want simply to do their job and then go away. Which is exactly what you should want of them. The fact is, many of the ads you've approved may have been written and art directed by free-lancers and their rates marked up by your agency.

But what about the other disciplines: media, research and account management?

Media planning and buying services are plentiful and every bit as good as agency media departments. Most research has always been done by outside firms employed by the agency, so that's no problem. The final piece in the puzzle has only recently come into play, the free lance account manager.

Here's still another advantage to working this way: people inside agencies tend to think of the bottom line as something far away that doesn't directly affect them; free lancers are constantly aware and solicitous of both yours and theirs.

Are there really top-notch creative people in the free-lance market? You bet. Just to mention a few, there's Dan Mountain, formerly of Hal Riney and Associates, in Santa Monica, Gary Brahl, former executive Creative Director of GSD&M, in Kansas City, and David Lyday, formerly of BBDO, New York, and DDB Needham, in Dallas, These three are as good or better than anyone currently working in any ad agency anywhere, with the sole exception of Hal Riney, himself.

Starting a virtual agency requires work but it's no more painful than sitting through agency presentations. You'll need a marketing director and an advertising coordinator on your end. They can start making phone calls, interviewing free-lancers for the various positions. A good free-lance art director can recommend several excellent free-lance writers, and vice versa. In turn, they can recommend a savvy media buyer and account manager. Rather than have an agency assign them to you, you'll be able to interview and choose them yourself. Bring them in as a group and work out a compensation system that's satisfactory for all. Then go to work, creating ads on the computer and sharing files on the Internet. Using the same disciplines you demand of any agency. And watch the cost of everything from printing to tape dubs go down.

Now you're close to operating at 100 percent.

XV

How To Judge Creative

One of the toughest jobs the client has to face is to judge the efficacy of the creative presented to her. Some, unaware of the sensitivities involved, rush headlong into the task like a kid running into a candy store. In this case, the metaphor can quickly shift to a bull in a china shop. To avoid this, recognize that most opinions regarding creative are entirely subjective, that the creative people possess a unique talent and therefore should be taken very seriously, and listen. Mostly listen.

Long before seeing creative, you should have bought off on a marketing strategy. I also recommend a creative strategy, a document that was once called a copy platform, before proceeding to copy and layouts or storyboards. Here's an interesting way to start people toward a creative strategy:

Draw a square and divide it into four parts. Write the word "emotional" at the top of the square and the word "intellectual" at the bottom. Then write "high price" on the left side of the square and "low cost" at the right side. Now ask everyone to choose the place your product or service should fall within the overall window. Is the consumer's buying decision based more on emotion or reason? Is it an expensive or relatively cheap product? Complex, high-priced items should generally fall in the lower left quadrant. Computers would be a good example, with Macintosh products moving more toward the center. Don't think of "intellectual" as dull. You can create intellectual excitement as well as emotional excitement. Automobiles are an interesting exception; while they are high priced, they create a lot of emotional excitement.

Remember, this is a game that is intended to stimulate thinking, not to make rules.

After you've reached something similar to consensus, draw the same window and position your product or service within your own industry. For example, as an automobile, a Toyota Corolla is an expensive purchase for people who are careful with their money. This puts it in the lower right quadrant. However, move it to an auto industry window and it moves diagonally. So who is your target audience, someone searching for an economical car right now, or someone who may be buying sometime in the distant future? Play the game. Get everyone thinking. Then, finally, agree on a spot, a position, on the window. Explain it to everyone's satisfaction in a written creative strategy. Then challenge the creative people to give it life.

Creative people should also be challenged to see the product or service from the consumers point of view. A Toyota is not a car to its owner. It's a friend and family member serving a critical transportation need. It must transport him and, while doing so, protect him and his family. That makes it far more than just a car. Think of it in the same light as the difference between laying bricks and building a house. What is the *meaning* of the product from the consumer's point of view?

These are guides, not rules. Richard Pruitt used to say that our boss, David Ogilvy, laid down his instructions for the guidance of wise men and the obedience of fools. Think of these in the same way; suggestions to help fuel creative thought.

Beware fads and fashion.

Predictably, advertising passes through fads like any other business. There was a time when no one used script. A decade later it was back in fashion. Once type was so closely kerned that it was hard to read. Thankfully, that's changed, too. There was a time when music was predominant in television commercials. Now, no one is doing it. To make matters worse, it all may have changed by the time you read this.

It's important to be aware of what is fashionable for one major reason: so you can avoid it.

Ads and commercials that do not cater to fashion do not make it into awards shows. They also do not look like every other ad and commercial out there.

Don't go with trends. Set trends.

Don't go with your agency's look. Go with your own look.

I once saw a free-lance production artist preparing to work on an incoming ad for a major national agency. She was setting up a series of boxes on her computer screen. Why? I asked. Because, she said, this agency always does layouts with boxes in them; she was getting ready to deliver their "look."

Be sure you're not stuck in a box.

Your customers won't buy a technique.

Years ago, Stan Freberg extolled the advantages of radio as an advertising medium by producing a commercial in which Lake Michigan was drained and refilled with hot chocolate topped by a mountain of whipped cream and a 10-ton cherry. Can't do that on television, he said.

Well, now you can. It's not cheap but it is possible. Computer animators and machines are pushing the word "impossible" out of the creative lexicon. This is great news, but like all great news, it has a severe downside, that being that technique can take over a commercial. It can become its own reason for being. Strategy is ignored, demographics be damned, we can show dinosaurs jumping rope and playing Frisbee. Consumers love this stuff. They remember every detail, except who the commercial is for.

Humor works...if it's funny.

Claude Hopkins said that no one wants to buy something from a clown. David Ogilvy agreed then later recanted. In a Gallup and Robinson presentation in 1973, the research firm announced the humor was the best way to get your commercial remembered. Now come the big ifs:

If the humor is funny to the consumer. Commercials that are hilarious to creative people in their 20's may totally miss an target audience in their 40's.

If the humor somehow revolves around product benefits. Telling a joke and then adding an "oh. by the way, eat at Burger Doodle," doesn't work.

If it's on strategy but it scares you, buy it.

Ogilvy talked about commercials that were so boring they passed like ships in the night. Even well wrought commercials that deliver the strategy effectively can be forgettable if they don't have something that rivets the viewer. It is that riveting piece, so often missing, that tends to scare clients. If your pulse jumps and the scared little person within you says "kill it!" do just the opposite.

Music can make all the difference.

I couldn't figure out why so many younger creative people disdained the use of music, and then it struck me: they don't know enough about it and are unwilling to learn. The fact is, music can make or break a commercial. Leaving it out is like serving the duck without the sauce. Here are some things I've learned about using it wisely.

Singing your product benefits will sound silly. Once my Hispanic compatriots on Sea World were playing a Spanish jingle they had recently recorded. The music was stirring, the singer passionate. The music swelling to a climax on a particular phrase, "tantos penquinos!" Certain that it was a heart-rending moment, I asked my Spanish speaking peers what it meant.

"Lots of penguins," they answered.

I laughed, and I imagine most Spanish-speaking people who heard the commercial laughed as well. It's not good to be laughed *at*, especially when humor is the last thing you're reaching for.

Think of music as an added element in setting the mood and adding to the emotional persuasion. Think of singing as music with voices added. Insist on lyrics that enforce the emotional, not the intellectual, appeal. Don't think a song is going to be a substitute for a concept or an idea. It's not. It is something that grows out of an idea.

People who have worked eight hours and come home to watch television are not interested in hearing a commercial that sounds like Nine Inch Nails. So don't waste your time, and money, being overly hip.

What about small budgets?

My friend Ben Morris at the MQ&C Agency in Austin has a "worthy cause," he works to find ways for small advertisers to afford television. He does it by planning carefully, buying 15-second spots on a highly opportunistic basis and insisting on effective creative. I believe there is a Ben Morris in most markets. All you have to do is find him, or her or them.

Sure it's good, but is it you?

Michael Blair at GSD&M does commercials for Wal-Mart that are not hip or cool and are not in the running for major awards. But they work. They really work. And they do so because Wal-Mart is not hip or cool. Mike does commercials that capture the spirit and soul of the people who work and shop at Wal-Mart. Director Rocky Powell, who does not live in Beverly Hills and does not ask a day rate the size of the national debt, manages to get these people, real people instead of actors, to be themselves.

Yes, you may say, but those commercials are so corny. Are they? Aren't they really just simple and honest? Aren't they really just lacking in pretense?

It takes courage to make commercials that render the product, store or service as it is, rather than try to make it appear as the creative people wish it were.

Most people are not hip or cool and have no desire to be. They like Wal-Mart and they like Wal-Mart commercials.

Here's the television production advice I promised in an earlier chapter: make sure your agency knows about the less-expensive directors and production companies, many of them outside the Los Angeles market. There are commercials that need and deserve expensive production. Most do not. Many times, your creative people are simply hoping a good director can save their mediocre idea. Don't go for it. Go over reels from less expensive sources with your agency and critique them together. If your agency can't find a less expensive director and production company, call me, and I will. But if you've approved an idea that requires a top shelf director, be ready to spend what it takes.

LAST TIP: Be yourself. As Hal Riney says, be genuine. Don't become what someone else thinks you should be. Hold strongly to your values. Stick to your mission. Make serving your customers into a worthy cause and pursue it with passion. Never settle for less than 100 percent!

www.ingramcontent.com/pod-product-compliance
Lightning Source LLC
Chambersburg PA
CBHW030841180526
45163CB00004B/1405